the best of

Barbie®

four decades of America's favorite doll

sharon korbeck

Published by

krause
publications

700 E. State Street, Iola, WI 54990-0001
Telephone: 715/445-2214
www.krause.com

Please call or write for our free catalog of publications. Our toll-free number to place an order or to obtain a free catalog is 800-258-0929 or please use our regular business telephone, 715-445-2214.

Library of Congress Catalog Number: 2001088586
ISBN: 0-87349-261-7

Printed in the United States of America

on the cover: *Pictured are Barbie dolls spanning four decades of an American classic. Pictured from left to right are Dream Date Barbie (1980s), which epitomizes the excesses of that decade; Lingerie Barbie (2000), which brings Barbie back to her glamorous roots; Color Magic Barbie (1960s), a decidedly bold introduction in a decade of change; and Malibu Barbie (1970s), which represented the sunny fresh-faced, long-haired look of the 1970s.*

tableofcontents

acknowledgments

Somewhere in Door County, Wisconsin, in a unassuming warehouse cleverly hidden off Hwy. 42/57, reside 2,000 Barbie dolls.

During the summer tourist season, the dolls stand at attention waiting for the visitors to come in, wide-eyed, and exclaim, "I had that doll!" Or for little girls to squeal, "Mommy, look at all the Barbie dolls!" Or for collectors to stand back and admiringly say, "What an outstanding collection."

It is for those three groups – the nostalgic fans, the young dreamers and the avid collectors — that this book is dedicated. And it is because of Georgia Rankin, owner of the epic collection you see in this book, that we were able to create *The Best of Barbie Doll*.

And so, thank you Georgia, for allowing us to photograph and document your enviable collection. You are a kind soul and an impassioned collector.

Krause Publications photographer Kris Kandler is, in my opinion, the MVP on this project. Her easy demeanor tempered a long photo shoot, and her keen photographic talents created the outstanding images in this book. Editor Dan Stearns remained a constant support, from his enthusiasm at the photo shoot to his sharp wit that kept me going to his prowess in enhancing the flavor of the text.

Thanks also to Rick Jones, for his continuing literary inspiration; to graphic designer Joe Perz for maintaining the theme of "best" in his cover and page design artistry; and to my associates in the Krause Publications toy/antiques division for picking up the slack while I worked on this project.

Thanks to my contacts at Mattel for their assistance and to Sandi Holder at Sandi Holder's Doll Attic in Union City, California for her help as well.

This book is dedicated to my sister, Kathy Gerbers, and my nieces Abby and Alaina Gerbers, whose love of Barbie dolls inspired me to write the best book possible.

Sharon Korbeck
March 2001

left: *Growing Up Skipper, released in 1977.*

what's best?

Hasn't everything already been written about Barbie? Haven't we seen all the photos? Learned all the variations?

While a search of the Library of Congress database uncovers more than 400 entries under "Barbie," no book has ever taken the organizational approach you see here. Quite simply, this book aims, in organization and content, to present "the best" of Barbie. *The Best of Barbie Doll* is not a completist compendium but rather a subjective exploration of the best dolls from 1959 to 2000.

Narrowing down our selection became easier when we finally defined "best." To collectors, "best" doesn't necessarily mean most valuable, best dressed or most influential. Best might simply mean the doll they love the most.

We took a broad, yet decidedly targeted, approach. The dolls listed in this book are included for one or more of the following reasons:

Influence, Import, Innovation. Some of the dolls are included because they are influential or important to the toy industry (like Ponytail #1), society (Black Francie), pop culture (Rocker Barbie) or collecting (Happy Holidays). Others take into account innovations such as Miss Barbie's sleep eyes or later dolls' talking capabilities.

Controversy. Inciting controversy from her inception, Barbie has faced many challenges in more than 40 years. These dolls are included under our "Best

> Best (best) adj. 1. Exceeding all others in excellence, achievement or quality: most excellent. 2. Most satisfactory, suitable, or useful: most desirable. 3. To the greatest extent or degree: Most.

Banter" section, examining the trials and tribulations you can endure . . . even if you are just an inanimate (albeit influential) vinyl doll.

Trends. The life of the Barbie doll has been cleverly cluttered with trends, for better or worse. Some of the best of these (like Bob Mackie fashions, swirl ponytail hair) are presented here.

When we were introduced to Georgia Rankin's awe-inspiring collection of more than 2,000 Barbie dolls in Northern Wisconsin, we knew we had the best to choose from. So it seemed natural to corral the dolls in this book under that encompassing heading.

So, aside from being an intriguing and colorful guide to the best of Barbie dolls for the past 42 years, this book will also serve the collector in these ways:

Values. A price guide at the back of the book provides up-to-date pricing for the dolls listed in this book, and many more.

ID Guide. Clear, full-color photos (many full-page examples), close-ups and accompanying text provide unquestionable identification for the dolls.

Glossary. You've seen phrases and abbreviations used in ads or other books, but do you know what they mean? Our concise, illustrated glossary is a handy inclusion.

above: *Fashion Model Lingerie #1.*
right: *Malibu Barbie.*

Georgia Rankin and her husband used to wake up every morning with literally hundreds of dolls in their bedroom. And these were just some of the favorites.

Thanks to Georgia, the Rankins' bedroom was a haven for vintage Barbie dolls . . . those that wouldn't fit into their already full Showcase Doll and Car Museum in Sturgeon Bay, Wisconsin.

When she recently sold the dolls in their bedroom (the entire grouping brought around $10,000), Georgia was left with a 2,000 Barbie dolls – a collection larger than just about anyone's in the

left: *Georgia Rankin, owner of the Showcase Museum in Sturgeon, Wisconsin, surrounded by Bob Mackie Barbie dolls.*
above: *Some of Georgia's homemade cases show off her vast collection.*

nation, except for, perhaps, Mattel's corporate archives.

"I look at so many, and I think, 'That's my favorite,'" said 70-year-old Georgia Rankin, a dealer/collector whose passion led her to create an unassuming and almost-hidden museum, home to thousands of Barbie dolls, other vintage dolls, animatronic store displays, action figures and classic automobiles. But Barbie dolls predominate.

left: *Virtually every doll, in every outfit for every season.*
right: *Ready for a close-up? Another view of the Barbie doll environments Georgia creates for her museum.*

It wasn't always that way. Rankin's true interest has always been larger antique dolls by manufacturers such as Simon and Halbig, Kestner, and Armand Marseilles. Looming in tall glass cases designed by Rankin, the dolls keep watch over their younger, hipper and more slender counterparts. Years ago when Rankin started her museum, she only had five or six Barbie dolls on display. And she seemed almost surprised when visitors, intrigued by the antique dolls, frequently inquired about the Barbie dolls. They wanted to see more.

And so it began.

Familiar with the Barbie dolls her two daughters used to play with in the 1960s, Rankin turned her focus to collecting Barbie dolls . . . all of them.

That was her goal, and now, decades later, Rankin has succeeded and then some. By her count, she owns every Barbie doll and fashion ever made by Mattel. And there's little evidence to dispute that claim.

"Once I started, I just went crazy. I bought them at rummage sales and doll shows. They used to be much easier to find," she said.

But aside from its inherent value and completeness, the collection inspires interest because of its "down-to-earth" presentation and accessibility.

One might expect a collection that valuable and complete to be housed in a pretentious marble-floored domain. The Showcase Museum is more of a windowless warehouse, really. Due to Sturgeon Bay city restrictions, signage is at a minimum. But for the unknowing who enter, it hardly matters that the amenities are few. The dolls provide plenty of opulence and nostalgia.

Rankin, a former art teacher, put toil, time and tenderness into designing and hand-crafting displays that allow the dolls to take center stage.

Rankin constructed Plexiglas cases with handles, sturdy enough to tote the collection to programs, library displays and speeches. The loose dolls aren't just stored in the cases, though. Rankin has them posed in hand-painted dioramas.

The Ponytail family poses in front of a beach scene. Elegantly dressed dolls stroll down a shop-lined boulevard. Dolls of the World front a map-lined case. Winter-garbed dolls lounge in a snow-covered scene.

Delicate and often rare accessories, such as the wax fish from the Picnic Set (1959-1961) outfit or the petite paper map from Open Road (1961-1962), are miraculously present. These tiny treasures, often lost, forgotten or overlooked, make the realistic arrangements even more enticing.

The dolls are arranged chronologically, so visitors can easily track Barbie doll changes in style and design throughout time. Rankin knows the collection so well she can locate a doll, and recite interesting facts about it, at the mere drop of a name.

When you love all the dolls, as Rankin does, it's hard to select a favorite. For a while, Rankin said she wanted "every single bride that was ever made."

Asked to name a favorite she would never part with, Rankin quickly answered, "A Ponytail #1 in the Gay Parisienne outfit."

An elegant choice, indeed. It's easy to understand why her current favorites are the 1990s City Seasons dolls dressed in chic street clothes. "I'm a little tired of gowns," she said.

While visitors to the museum aren't permitted, of course, to handle the dolls, Rankin is refreshingly open about handling her own vintage treasures. She has no qualms about dressing the dolls, styling their hair, fixing their blemishes and reposing them for photos. They are, after all, made to be enjoyed to their fullest.

And that may be the best lesson learned after visiting Rankin and her museum. It's not about the number of dolls or even their value. It's about the long history of collecting, the history remembered, the nostalgic memories and the good times.

Rankin's Showcase Museum, located on Hwy. 42/57 in Sturgeon Bay, Wisconsin, is open May through December, in the middle of the active Door County tourist season. For more information, contact Georgia Rankin at 920-743-6788.

bestbeginnings

She's got a body to die for, and she goes by only one name. Who is this super-star? Madonna? Cher? It's none other than Mattel's Barbie doll.

And the world of Barbie doll today is much more than just a doll and accessories. Barbie doll has kept pace with society through disco and disasters, careers and computers.

Barbie doll's beginnings are well-documented; her birth happened smack in the middle of a strong 1950s postwar economy.

Back then, Americans liked "Ike" in the White House and Milton Berle on TV. *Ben-Hur* nabbed the Oscar for Best Picture. Teen idols like Fabian and Frankie Avalon elicited swoons from oceans of tender hearts.

Alaska and Hawaii joined the United States, and Detroit's new cars featured big, bold tailfins. Teenagers set trends by the music they listened to, the movies they watched and the clothes they wore. Little girls dressed up paper dolls and played make-believe with baby dolls.

It was then that the Barbie doll came as an inspiration to Mattel co-founder Ruth Handler as she watched her young daughter, Barbara, playing with paper dolls.

Barbara and her friends liked to play adult or teenage make-believe with the dolls, imagining them in roles as college students, cheerleaders and adults with careers.

Handler immediately recognized that playing and pretending about the future was an important part of growing up. In researching the marketplace, she discovered a void and was determined to fill the niche with a three-dimensional fashion doll. Her all-male design staff, however, harbored doubts.

Several designs later, Mattel introduced Barbie, the Teen-Age Fashion Model, to skeptical buyers at New York's annual Toy Fair in 1959. Never before had they seen a doll so completely unlike the baby and toddler dolls popular at the time. Undaunted, Mattel used innovative television advertising to reach its audience. Today, the Barbie doll empire is close to a $1.5 billion a year industry.

Over the years, Barbie doll has indeed achieved the title of most popular fashion doll ever created. She's held that title by adapting to the times . . .

right: *Ponytail #2, from 1959.*

while still remaining remarkably the same (at least in body, if not in garb).

With fashion and teenage lifestyle trends evolving at a startling rate, the hundreds of people who have worked to keep Barbie doll current have had their hands full as styles changed from Paris couture to the inspired elegance of the Jacqueline Kennedy years to a more free-flowing, youthful look.

Mattel's design and development staff have remained current by identifying trends that relate to the lives of American teenagers.

For instance, in 1964, The Beatles led the British Invasion, and along with a new sound, brought hemlines way up and hair way down as teenagers adopted the Carnaby Street look. Barbie doll went mod a few years later with new face sculpting in 1967, which brought her current with the next generation of little girls who adored her.

In the 1970s, Barbie dolls wore up-to-the-minute fashions reflecting the prairie look, the granny dress, the California Girl suntan craze and the glittery styles of the disco years. By the end of the decade, Barbie doll's face was again resculpted to a wide smile and sunstreaked hair that showcased the beauty trends of the day.

Mattel's design and development staff have remained current by identifying trends that relate to the lives of American teenagers.

In the 1980s, Barbie dolls kept current as an aerobics instructor, a briefcase-carrying power executive and a couture-inspired sophisticate reflecting the popularity of nighttime soap operas. In the late 1990s, the Barbie doll stepped into the world of women's sports as a member of the WNBA (Women's National Basketball Association) and as a NASCAR racer.

Finally, as the millennium turned, Barbie doll concurrently ran for president (the only undisputed winner!) and soared as a superhero (Wonder Woman).

Barbie dolls have been called an "evergreen" property, an adjective infrequently used in the toy industry. Far too often, toys and the whims of the fickle buying public are fleeting.

But unlike decades of toys lost in the attics of memory, Mattel's Barbie doll has surpassed probably even Ruth Handler's expectations.

above: *Dream Date Barbie.*
right: *Commuter Set—one of the most elegant early Barbie doll outfits.*

Talking P.J.

Model #1113
Hair Colors: Blond
Current Value: **$250 MIB**

word of the decade: change

"**B**arbie touches so many aspects of a girl's psyche from adventure to independence to dreams of aspirations, that the emotional connections with the Barbie brand run deep." [from *Creating Ever-Cool: A Marketer's Guide to a Kid's Heart* by Gene Del Vecchio.]

"Emotional connections." That phrase was written in the late 1990s about the Barbie doll, but it is the synergy that the doll has with its owners that has echoed true for more than 40 years. An emotional connection with a toy is perhaps the best thing a toymaker can hope for; that may be just what Ruth Handler had in mind. Creating that emotional connection didn't happen overnight, and it took a healthy dose of change to bring the doll to that point.

left: *P.J., introduced as a friend to Barbie doll, was just one of the many changes happening in the Barbie doll universe during the decade.*
right: *As is typical of the doll, her vinyl face has faded considerably. However, this Ponytail Barbie #1 still looks great over 40 years later.*

Ponytail #1

Model #850
Hair Colors: Blond, brunette
Current Value: **$9,000 MIB**

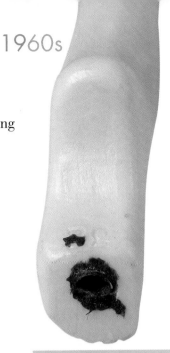

The first decade of Barbie doll was marked by change — change that proved necessary to keeping the doll fresh and foremost in the minds of little girls and retailers. When the face of the first doll was deemed too harsh or severe, Mattel kept tweaking it. And the changes continued. Just as 1960s women were turning to fashion magazines and the media for their cues, so was Barbie doll. Hair colors and styles were never static, and fashions were up-to-date and, often, ahead of the curve.

Change went beyond the cosmetic in the 1960s. Two of the more major changes in the doll's history — the Twist and Turn body and a talking mechanism — were introduced in the 1960s.

What would come next? Society, always an influence in Barbie doll history, would take over.

The Best Because?

Because they were the first Barbie dolls, Ponytails can easily be justified as the best, for without their creation, Barbie doll's future look may have been very different. Each variation may not have been the "best" example, but it's clear that by Ponytail #5, Mattel had succeeded in offering what would be the basic model for a classic.

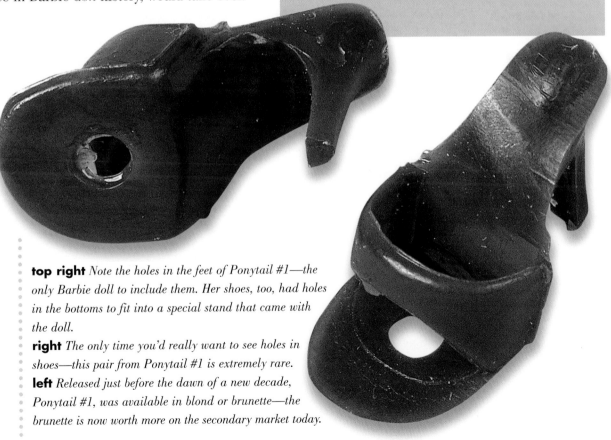

top right *Note the holes in the feet of Ponytail #1—the only Barbie doll to include them. Her shoes, too, had holes in the bottoms to fit into a special stand that came with the doll.*

right *The only time you'd really want to see holes in shoes—this pair from Ponytail #1 is extremely rare.*

left *Released just before the dawn of a new decade, Ponytail #1, was available in blond or brunette—the brunette is now worth more on the secondary market today.*

Looking Out For #1

To a beginning collector, the early Ponytail Barbie dolls may look similar, but there are subtle differences. Here are the features to look for when identifying a 1959 Ponytail Barbie #1:

• Holes in the bottom of the feet with copper tubes (holes were then used to insert the doll on a special stand)

• Zebra-stripe, one-piece swimsuit

• Blond or brunette ponytail hairdo with soft, curly bangs

• Red fingernails, toenails and lips

• Gold hoop earrings

• White irises of the eyes and severely arched eyebrows

• Side-glancing eyes

• Pale, almost white, ivory skin tone

• The original #1 dolls also came packaged with white sunglasses and black mules with holes in bottom

• Markings on buttocks read: "Barbie T.M./Pats.Pend/©MCMLVIII/by/Mattel/Inc."

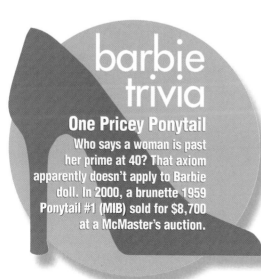

barbie trivia
One Pricey Ponytail
Who says a woman is past her prime at 40? That axiom apparently doesn't apply to Barbie doll. In 2000, a brunette 1959 Ponytail #1 (MIB) sold for $8,700 at a McMaster's auction.

Change would continue, but by the 1970s, Barbie doll was ready to be a leader, not a follower, of trends. She would be ready for action.

Ponytail Era

When Mattel sold over a quarter of a million of the very first Barbie doll in 1959, the company may have felt a twinge of encouragement.

But even though creator Ruth Handler had anticipated a success, that belief was not universal. So after the doll's debut, Mattel immediately began tweaking its creation — ushering in a decade of change for what would eventually become the most popular doll of all time.

right *Still showing off arched eyebrows and a similar face, Ponytail #2 did not include the holes in her feet that so mark the first doll.*

Ponytail #2

Model #850
Hair Colors: Blond, brunette
Current Value:**$7,000 MIB**

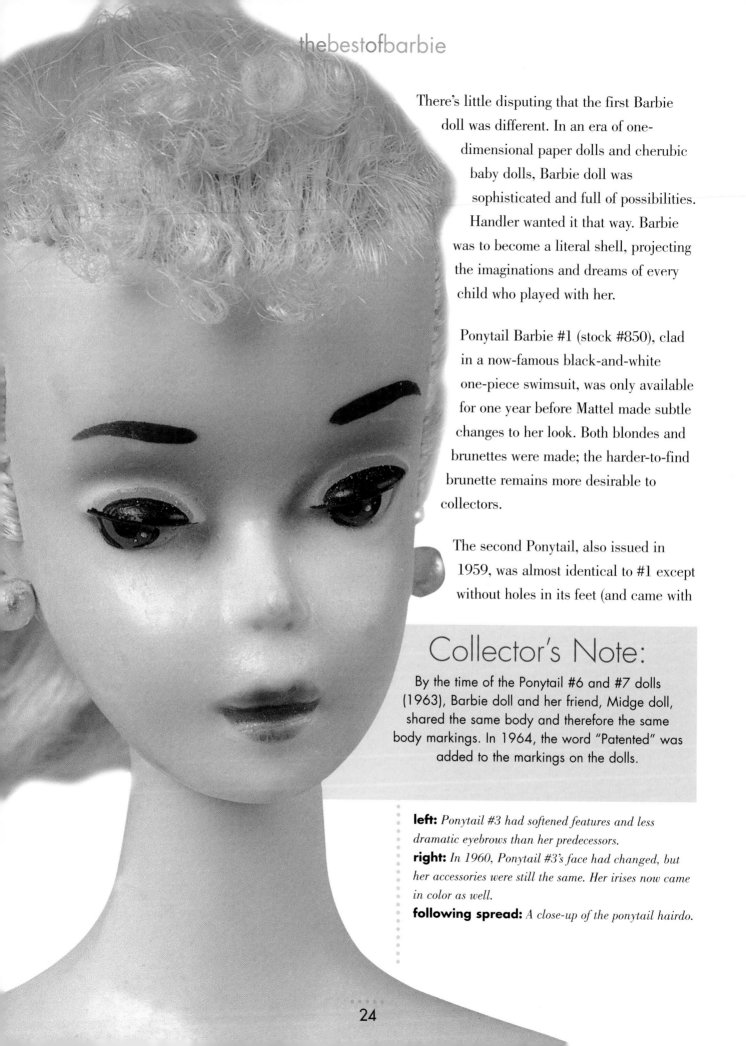

There's little disputing that the first Barbie doll was different. In an era of one-dimensional paper dolls and cherubic baby dolls, Barbie doll was sophisticated and full of possibilities. Handler wanted it that way. Barbie was to become a literal shell, projecting the imaginations and dreams of every child who played with her.

Ponytail Barbie #1 (stock #850), clad in a now-famous black-and-white one-piece swimsuit, was only available for one year before Mattel made subtle changes to her look. Both blondes and brunettes were made; the harder-to-find brunette remains more desirable to collectors.

The second Ponytail, also issued in 1959, was almost identical to #1 except without holes in its feet (and came with

Collector's Note:

By the time of the Ponytail #6 and #7 dolls (1963), Barbie doll and her friend, Midge doll, shared the same body and therefore the same body markings. In 1964, the word "Patented" was added to the markings on the dolls.

left: *Ponytail #3 had softened features and less dramatic eyebrows than her predecessors.*
right: *In 1960, Ponytail #3's face had changed, but her accessories were still the same. Her irises now came in color as well.*
following spread: *A close-up of the ponytail hairdo.*

Ponytail #3

Model #850
Hair Colors: Blond, brunette
Current Value:**$1,300 MIB**

a slightly different stand). Colorless eyes and severe eyebrows on both dolls gave them a slightly eerie appearance.

By 1960, the third variation (Ponytail #3) offered a softer face with muted makeup, blue eyes and gently curved eyebrows.

The Barbie doll face wasn't the only target of experimentation; at the same time, Mattel was also testing different vinyls. The waxy-smelling vinyl used for the first three dolls faded to a pale white over time.

With her fourth change in just two years, Ponytail Barbie #4 was issued in 1960 with the same face as #3 but a new, improved vinyl that retained its color.

By 1961, Barbie doll had matured, and Mattel apparently felt more comfortable with the more-defined look of the doll. The Ponytail Barbie #5 featured a lighter, hollow body. Titian, a reddish hair color, was introduced, and #5 was the first doll to wear a wrist tag.

Later Ponytails (#6 and #7) were made from 1962 to 1966 with varying hair, brow and lip colors.

left: *Ponytail #5.*
above: *Made with a new vinyl that was supposed to discourage color fading, Ponytail #5 dolls experience what can only be called "greasy face syndrome" over time.*
right: *Ponytail #5 was the first hollow-bodied Barbie doll.*

Ponytail #5

Model #850
Hair Colors: Blond, brunette, titian (red)
Current Value: **$400 MIB**

Bubblecut Barbie

(second issue, 1962 and later)
Model #850
Hair Colors: Blond, brunette, titian (red).
Shades of blond and brunette vary from very
pale blond to dark brownette
Current Value: **$350 MIB**

Bubblecuts Begin
(1961)

What's a girl to do? After enduring all the facelifts of 1959 and 1960, the Barbie doll adopted somewhat of a standard look. Once her look had mellowed in the Ponytail age, Barbie doll was yet to undergo more change.

In 1961, Barbie doll, although still delightfully perky in her ponytail, was given a alternate hairdo – a shorter, bouffant cut called the Bubblecut (dolls with ponytail hairdos, however, were still available until 1966).

By the Bubblecut era, Barbie doll had traded in her black-and-white swimsuit for a red one, and the hairstyle was offered in a variety of colors (blond, titian, brunette, brownette and variations) and styles (the side-part Bubblecut, with the hair combed to one side, is a valuable variation).

The Best Because?

Bubblecuts represent the first major hairstyle change for Barbie doll, an element that would be key to development over the next 40 years. The doll's chameleon attributes have often been connected to her coiffure.

left: *So much to do… this Bubblecut is all set in her "Busy Morning" sundress, a later version of "Suburban Shopper."*
right: *A new "do" became available in 1961, but some dolls still featured that same greasy face.*

Bubblecut Barbie

(first issue, 1961)
Model #850
Hair Colors: Blond, brunette, titian (red). Shades of blond and brunette vary from very pale blond to dark brownette
Current Value:**$1,400 MIB**

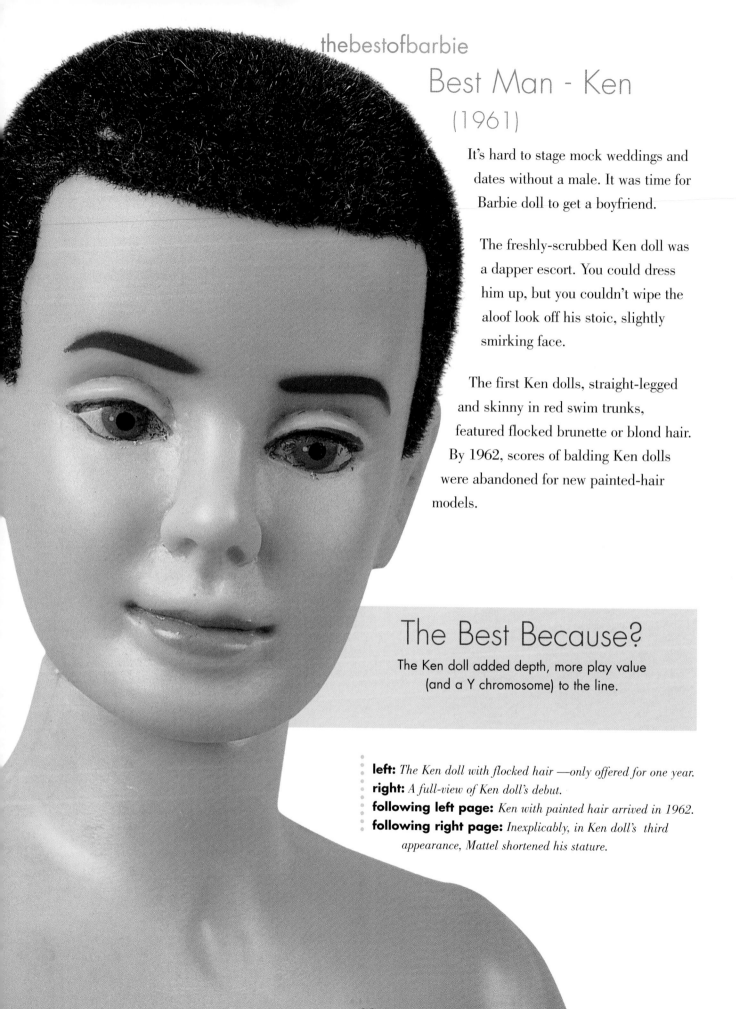

Best Man - Ken
(1961)

It's hard to stage mock weddings and dates without a male. It was time for Barbie doll to get a boyfriend.

The freshly-scrubbed Ken doll was a dapper escort. You could dress him up, but you couldn't wipe the aloof look off his stoic, slightly smirking face.

The first Ken dolls, straight-legged and skinny in red swim trunks, featured flocked brunette or blond hair. By 1962, scores of balding Ken dolls were abandoned for new painted-hair models.

The Best Because?

The Ken doll added depth, more play value (and a Y chromosome) to the line.

left: *The Ken doll with flocked hair —only offered for one year.*
right: *A full-view of Ken doll's debut.*
following left page: *Ken with painted hair arrived in 1962.*
following right page: *Inexplicably, in Ken doll's third appearance, Mattel shortened his stature.*

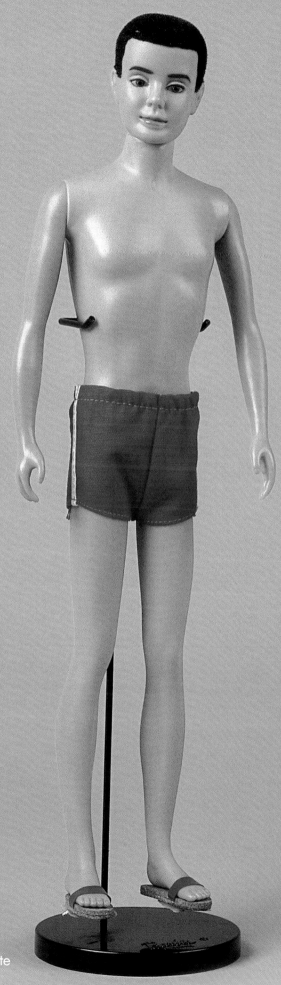

Ken

(first issue, flocked hair)
Model #750
Hair Colors: Blond or brunette
Current Value: **$200 MIB**

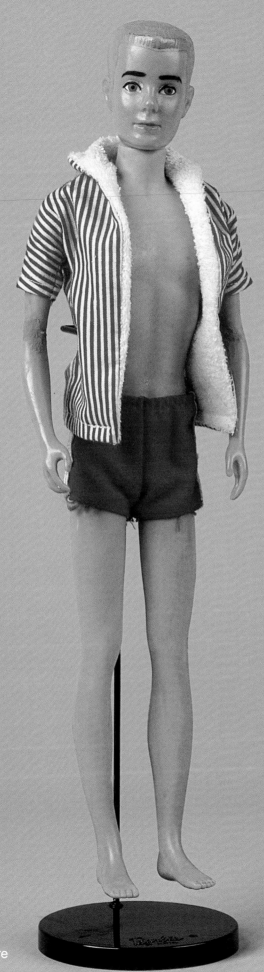

Ken
(first issue, painted hair)
Model #750
Hair Colors: Blond or brunette
Current Value: **$175 MIB**

Ken

(painted hair, 1962 shorter doll)
Model #750
Current Value: **$175 MIB**

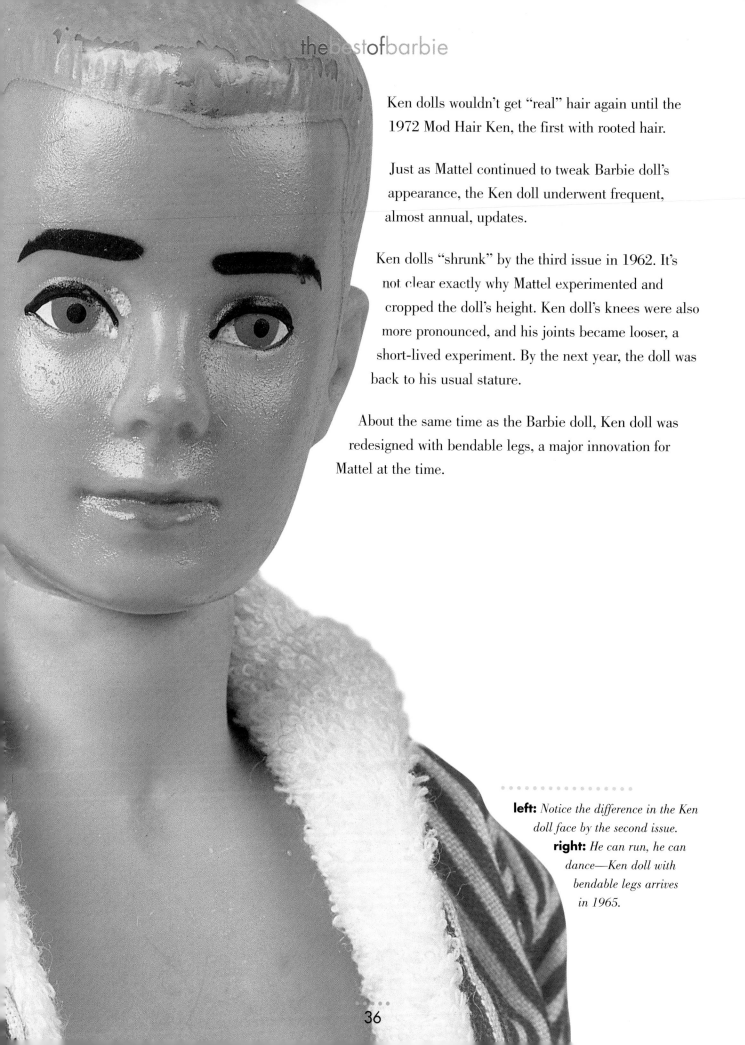

Ken dolls wouldn't get "real" hair again until the 1972 Mod Hair Ken, the first with rooted hair.

Just as Mattel continued to tweak Barbie doll's appearance, the Ken doll underwent frequent, almost annual, updates.

Ken dolls "shrunk" by the third issue in 1962. It's not clear exactly why Mattel experimented and cropped the doll's height. Ken doll's knees were also more pronounced, and his joints became looser, a short-lived experiment. By the next year, the doll was back to his usual stature.

About the same time as the Barbie doll, Ken doll was redesigned with bendable legs, a major innovation for Mattel at the time.

left: *Notice the difference in the Ken doll face by the second issue.*
right: *He can run, he can dance—Ken doll with bendable legs arrives in 1965.*

Ken

(bendable leg)
Model #1020
Hair Colors: Blond or brunette
Current Value: **$300 MIB**

Fashion Queen Barbie

Model #870
Hair Colors: Brown (painted)
Current Value: **$500 MIB**

Fashion Queen
(1963)

Her turban created the allure of Cleopatra. Uncovered, the doll's molded hair head looked otherworldly.

A mere four years old, Barbie doll had become a style trendsetter by 1963. Fashions and accessories were quickly becoming key to Barbie doll success. It was fitting, then, for Mattel to introduce Fashion Queen. Dressed in a gold and white striped swimsuit, Fashion Queen wore a matching turban to cover her molded hair – a first for the doll. Wigs included with the set allowed Fashion Queen to transform her hair from blond bubblecut to red flip to brunette pageboy.

eerie......but true......

Plenty of little boys may have pulled the heads off their sisters' Barbie dolls. The Fashion Queen Wig Wardrobe set may have inspired some girls to try that themselves. Sold separately from the doll, the Wig Wardrobe included three wigs and just the head of Fashion Queen. This allowed kids to mix and match dolls, heads and hairstyles. Spooky.

left: *In 1963, Fashion Queen Barbie appeared, signaling a new emphasis on hairstyling. She actually came with painted hair, and it was up to the kids to decide whether she should go with one of the wigs or just the glamorous turban.*

The Best Because?

Unlike any doll before her, Fashion Queen came in unique packaging with her own accessories – three wigs. It had become evident that Barbie doll hair was the focal point of her play value. That fact only intensified throughout the doll's lifetime.

Swirl Ponytail
(1964)

Stylish. That adjective epitomizes the elegance of Barbie doll's new Swirl Ponytail hairstyle for 1964. The common bangs found on earlier Ponytails were replaced with a soft sweep of hair. Variations are endless; dolls have been found with engaging White Ginger (platinum) or lemony yellow hair; lip color also varies widely, from red and coral to white and almost lavender.

The Best Because?

This doll's elegance was unparalleled for its time. Not only was the hairstyle chic, but a new wave of eye-catching colors for hair and lips added interest and impact.

left: *In 1964, the Swirl Ponytail arrived in almost every possible variation.*
right: *Originally, Swirl Ponytail wore a red one-piece swimsuit. Pictured here, she has borrowed one from American Girl.*

Swirl Ponytail

Model #850
Hair Colors: Blond, brunette, titian and variant
colors of platinum blond and lemon yellow
Current Value: **$625 MIB**

Miss Barbie
Model #1060
Hair Colors: Brown (painted)
Current Value: **$1,200 MIB**

Miss Barbie
(1964)

There's a reason this unusual-looking doll had a faraway glance . . . and the eyes have it. This innovative doll was the first (and last) Barbie doll to have "sleep eyes" that opened and closed. Because of this, her head was plastic, not soft vinyl.

Designed as a beach beauty in pink glittery swimsuit and cap, Miss Barbie could hardly romp on the sand without another innovation – bendable legs.

Without her shower cap, the molded-hair Miss Barbie could get wigged out, just like her predecessor, Fashion Queen. But beware – cap or wigs left on the doll's hard-plastic head too long could cause "melt marks."

The Best Because?

Major innovation (even though it was never used again). Wigs galore. Unique packaging. Cool shower cap.

left: *Like Fashion Queen, the Miss Barbie doll came with painted hair that practically begged to have a wig put on it.*
below: *Dig that crazy shower cap. The one pictured is not original, but darn close.*

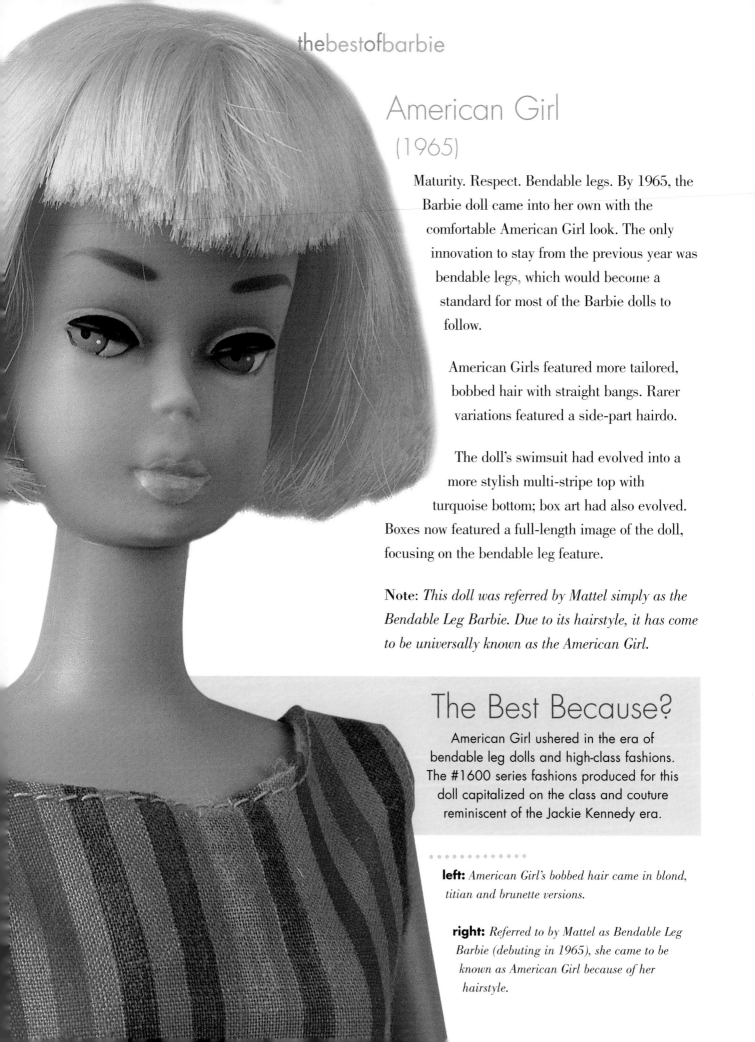

American Girl
(1965)

Maturity. Respect. Bendable legs. By 1965, the Barbie doll came into her own with the comfortable American Girl look. The only innovation to stay from the previous year was bendable legs, which would become a standard for most of the Barbie dolls to follow.

American Girls featured more tailored, bobbed hair with straight bangs. Rarer variations featured a side-part hairdo.

The doll's swimsuit had evolved into a more stylish multi-stripe top with turquoise bottom; box art had also evolved. Boxes now featured a full-length image of the doll, focusing on the bendable leg feature.

Note: *This doll was referred by Mattel simply as the Bendable Leg Barbie. Due to its hairstyle, it has come to be universally known as the American Girl.*

The Best Because?

American Girl ushered in the era of bendable leg dolls and high-class fashions. The #1600 series fashions produced for this doll capitalized on the class and couture reminiscent of the Jackie Kennedy era.

left: *American Girl's bobbed hair came in blond, titian and brunette versions.*

right: *Referred to by Mattel as Bendable Leg Barbie (debuting in 1965), she came to be known as American Girl because of her hairstyle.*

American Girl

(first issue, 1965)
Model #1070
Hair Colors: Blond, brunette, titian
and variant colors of platinum
blond and light yellow
Current Value: **$1,900 MIB**

Color Magic

Model #1150
Hair Colors: Golden Blonde/Scarlet Flame; Midnight/Ruby Red
Current Value: **$2,400 — $3,500 MIB**

Color Magic
(1966)

Future alchemists and hairdressers could have learned their trades with this creative doll. If it wasn't enough for girls to dress and accessorize their dolls, now they could dye their dolls' hair.

The innovative color-changing solution was mild, yet effective enough to create magical effects.

Two long-haired versions (with side-part hair) were available; Golden Blonde hair could change to Scarlet Flame (and back again) and Midnight could change to Ruby Red. The doll's diamond print swimsuit would also change colors when swabbed with the solution.

Midnight Mint:

Dolls with Midnight hair (that hasn't faded to red) are especially rare. Expect to pay $2,000 or more for such a Mint in Box example.

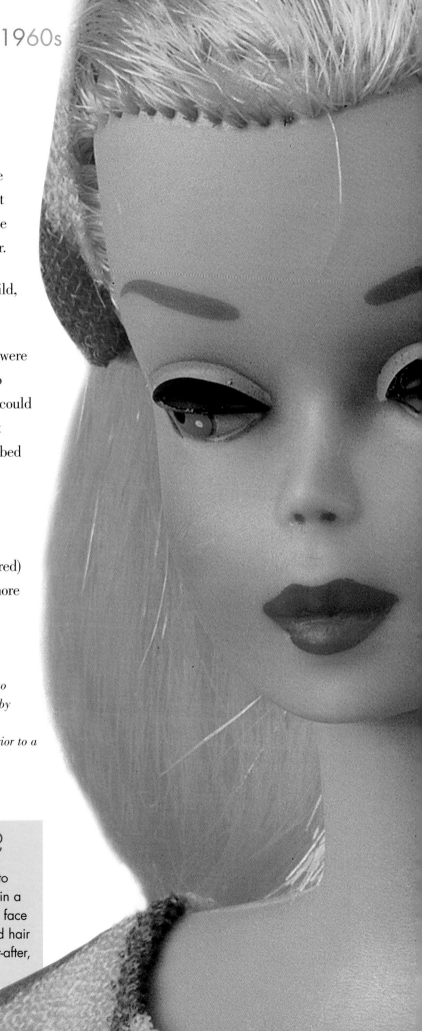

left: *A solution turned Golden Blonde hair to Scarlet Flame and Midnight changed to Ruby Red. So easy!*
right: *As gold as it gets—Golden Blonde prior to a Scarlet Flame transformation.*

The Best Because?

Color Magic was one of the earliest dolls to embrace the idea of hair play, and it did so in a way that was unique for its time. A high color face strong enough to compete with drop-dead bold hair has made Color Magic one of the most sought-after, and valuable, dolls today.

Twist and Turn Barbie
(1967)

Often known as "TNT," these dolls lived up to their name. They were a dynamite addition to the previously static dolls offered with straight or bendable legs. A pivoting waist added play value and poseability beyond compare.

TNTs packed a one-two punch of modernism into a small package. Not only did Barbie doll's body change, her look was softened. As the first doll with rooted eyelashes, TNT Barbie featured eyes as dramatic as those of Twiggy, the famous British model, (Mattel also made a Twiggy doll in 1967, its first doll based on a real person).

The Barbie doll's flowing straight locks got a boost in color, and for the first time, her super-shiny hair was given a description. Hair wasn't just blond, brunette or titian. Now it was Summer Sand, Go Go Co Co, Sun Kissed or Chocolate Bon Bon.

Ship Me a TNT ASAP:

In a noteworthy marketing move, Mattel initiated a trade-in promotion for the popular TNT dolls. Mattel offered to trade a new TNT doll to those who shipped the company their old Barbie doll plus $1.50. Kind of an early upgrade. The trade-in dolls were identical to regular TNTs, but they were packaged in a specially-marked box.

The Best Because?

There's no doubt this was a turning point doll for Mattel. It signaled a departure from the doll's earlier more staunch, proper look. The forces of pop culture began to take hold; that would continue throughout Barbie doll history. Never before had outside influences so infiltrated Barbie doll fashions, attitude, even body style. Mattel's "teen-age fashion model" was growing up in a bustling decade . . . and there was no turning back now.

left: *Rooted eyelashes, a softer-edged face and great locks.*
right: *Ready for the go-go—Twist and Turn Barbie swivels onto the scene in 1967—the first Barbie doll that could turn at the waist.*

Twist and Turn

Model #1160
Hair Colors: Blond, brunette, titian
Current Value: **$500 MIB**

Talking Barbie
Model #1115
Hair Colors: Blond, brunette, titian
Current Value: **$425 MIB**

Talking Barbie
(1968)

For nine years, Barbie dolls had been mute – a vessel in which little girls could channel their emotions, thoughts and speech. But the late 1960s had spawned a new technology that Mattel was currently using in other toys – a talking mechanism.

Not exactly a Chatty Cathy, Talking Barbie (with the mod TNT body and a pullstring on her back) chatted of fashion, dates, the prom, shopping and parties.

left: *Late-1960s technology gave Barbie doll a voice with a new "talking" model.*
right: *Talking Barbie could opine about the latest teen fashions, the fun upcoming prom and a variety of age-appropriate subjects.*

The Best Because?

Using the technology of the time, Talking Barbie was yet another mod-era example of how changing times influenced the doll's development. It's a treat for collectors, too, to hear a vintage talker that can still speak.

51

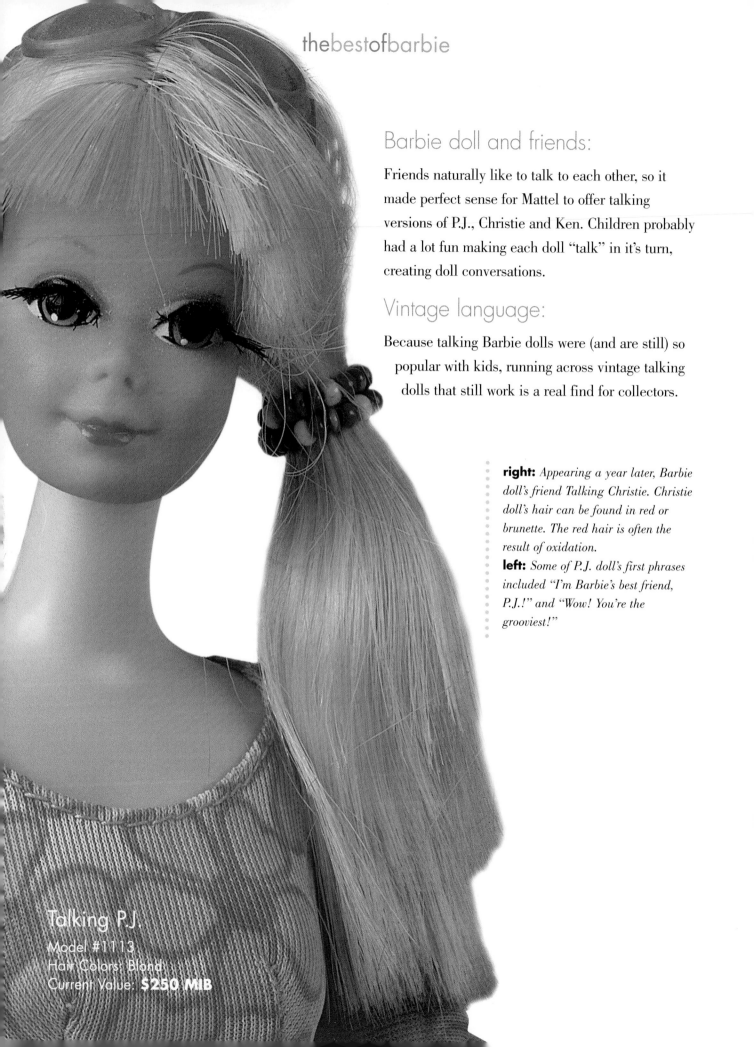

Barbie doll and friends:

Friends naturally like to talk to each other, so it made perfect sense for Mattel to offer talking versions of P.J., Christie and Ken. Children probably had a lot fun making each doll "talk" in it's turn, creating doll conversations.

Vintage language:

Because talking Barbie dolls were (and are still) so popular with kids, running across vintage talking dolls that still work is a real find for collectors.

right: *Appearing a year later, Barbie doll's friend Talking Christie. Christie doll's hair can be found in red or brunette. The red hair is often the result of oxidation.*

left: *Some of P.J. doll's first phrases included "I'm Barbie's best friend, P.J.!" and "Wow! You're the grooviest!"*

Talking P.J.
Model #1113
Hair Colors: Blond
Current Value: **$250 MIB**

Se Habla Espanol:

To expand Barbie doll's audience, Mattel also marketed Talking Barbie in a Spanish-speaking version in the 1960s. As the years passed, Barbie dolls were released that could speak many languages, including French, German, Dutch and Italian.

barbie trivia

All in the Family
Ruth and Elliot Handler, founders of Mattel, didn't have to go far to come up with their dolls' names. They were named after their children, Barbara and Ken.

Talking Christie.
Model #1126
Hair Colors: Reddish Brown or brunette
Current Value: **$200 MIB**

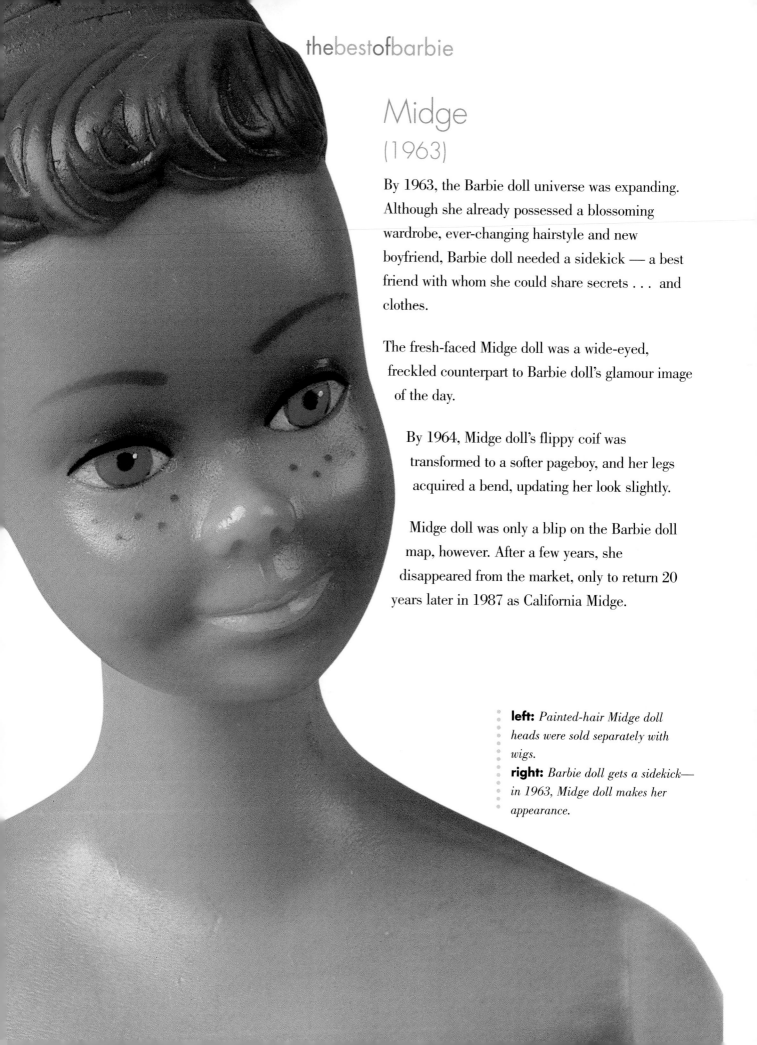

Midge
(1963)

By 1963, the Barbie doll universe was expanding. Although she already possessed a blossoming wardrobe, ever-changing hairstyle and new boyfriend, Barbie doll needed a sidekick — a best friend with whom she could share secrets . . . and clothes.

The fresh-faced Midge doll was a wide-eyed, freckled counterpart to Barbie doll's glamour image of the day.

By 1964, Midge doll's flippy coif was transformed to a softer pageboy, and her legs acquired a bend, updating her look slightly.

Midge doll was only a blip on the Barbie doll map, however. After a few years, she disappeared from the market, only to return 20 years later in 1987 as California Midge.

left: *Painted-hair Midge doll heads were sold separately with wigs.*
right: *Barbie doll gets a sidekick— in 1963, Midge doll makes her appearance.*

Midge
(first issue, straight leg)
Model #860
Hair Colors: Blond, brunette, titian
Current Value:**$175 MIB**

Midge
(bendable leg)
Model #1080
Hair Colors: Blond, brunette, titian
Current Value: **$425 MIB**

Rarity Alert:

Watch for rare variations
of Midge dolls, including
those sans freckles and
those with painted teeth.

Heads Up:

Even though Midge dolls
projected a perkier face to the
world, Midge dolls and Barbie dolls
are exactly alike aside from their
heads. Original straight-legged Midge
dolls had the same body and markings as
Fashion Queen Barbie. It's only
appropriate, then, that painted hair Midge
doll heads were also sold with a wig
wardrobe set.

The Best Because?

Midge doll provided a much-needed youthful
counterpart to Barbie doll and was the first of Mattel's
efforts to expand Barbie doll's friends and family.

left: *In 1964, Midge grew out a soft
pageboy do and her legs could bend.*

Skipper
(first issue, straight leg)
Model #950
Hair Colors: Blond, brunette, titian
Current Value: **$195 MIB**

Skipper
(1964)

Friends are important, but nothing's more solid than family ties. Barbie doll's first family member, little sister Skipper, arrived in 1964. Wearing a red-and-white sailor swimsuit, the doe-eyed Skipper doll was unique in stature. She was 9 inches tall, a little shorter than her big sister, but packed with personality. Most of her early fashions were pint-sized versions of Barbie doll's couture, but she looked more at home in her very own jaunty apparel, splashed with plaids, flowers, spots and lace.

Later issues of Skipper doll featured bendable leg and twist-and-turn versions.

Brass Bandit:

Got a Skipper doll with green hair? It may not be just a fashion faux pas. Original Skipper dolls came adorned with a brass headband. Left in, the brass can oxidize, causing the hair around it to turn green. Still, the headbands remain a coveted commodity. Collectors might pay $20 for a vintage headband to complete their doll's ensemble.

The Best Because?

She was the first member of Barbie doll's immediate family. She also ushered in a more youthful, playful era of sidekick dolls, like Skipper doll's friend Skooter doll.

left: *Lil' Sis… Skipper doll was a little shorter than her big sister, so borrowing clothes was out of the question.*

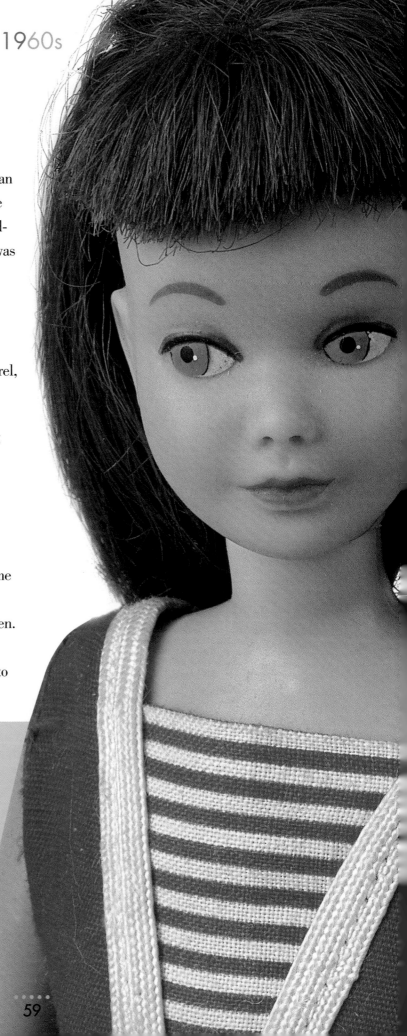

The End of Innocence:

A most wholesome introduction, Skipper doll skipped unobtrusively through an entire decade. However, by the mid-1970s, Mattel introduced the Growing Up Skipper doll. One twist of Skipper doll's arms caused her bustline to grow, transforming her from girl to teenager just like that! If only it were so simple.

barbie trivia

Which of the following sports associations has not been represented by a Barbie doll? Major League Baseball Women's National Basketball Association National Hockey League NASCAR

Answer: Mattel has not made a National Hockey League doll . . . yet.

right: *Later versions of Skipper doll featured bendable legs.*
below: *Skipper doll's wardrobe wasn't the only nautical theme in the Barbie doll universe—check out Ken doll's cool boat.*

Skipper

(bendable leg)
Model #1030
Hair Colors: Blond, brunette, titian
Current Value: **$250 MIB**

The Best Because?

Simply due to their unique size and bodies, Todd and Tutti dolls introduced yet another innovation to the Barbie doll line. Did it succeed? Few dolls went on to exhibit these traits, but Todd and Tutti dolls (also available in a gift pack enjoying ice cream sundaes) are pint-sized reminders of Mattel's attempts to expand the family tree.

Todd and Tutti
(1965)

What a joyous day it must have been in the Barbie doll family when Barbie and Skipper doll's twin siblings arrived! Unusual in stature (these dolls were tiny!) and construction (they featured bendy bodies with internal wires), Todd and Tutti were wide-eyed twins, alternately cherubic and a little odd with their unflinching, steely gazes. Neither were around very long, making them interesting and oft-forgotten family members to find today.

Unlike other members of the Barbie doll family, Todd and Tutti doll's poseable bodies featured internal wires designed to make their bodies bendy. Found today, the dolls' bodies may show signs of turning green, a result of the deterioration of metal wires inside the dolls.

right: *Todd and Tutti dolls, added to the line in 1965, expanded the Barbie doll family a little bit more. Tutti is weaing modified shoes, originally belonging to Barbie doll.*

Todd and Tutti
Model #3590 (Todd) and #3580 (Tutti)
Hair Colors: Titian
Current Value: Around **$200 each MIB**

Skooter
(1965)

Although Skipper doll's playmate had a Daisy Mae appearance, she was a wholesome, pug-nosed sprite with bouncy pigtails. A splash of freckles completed her mischievous look.

Note: *Skooter doll's hair originally was styled in pigtails.*

left: *Skooter doll was cute as a button, but short-lived, making her a favorite with collectors.* right: *Skooter doll… another friend, this time a pal for Skipper doll.*

64

Skooter

(first issue, straight leg)
Model #1040
Hair Colors: Blond, brunette, titian
Current Value: **$180 MIB**

Skooter

(bendable leg)
Model #1120
Hair Colors: Blond, brunette, titian
Current Value: **$350 MIB**

left: *In 1966, Skooter doll arrived on the scene with bendable legs*

below: *Looking fresh off the farm, Skooter doll in freckles and pigtails.*

The Best Because?

Cute as a button, Skooter doll remains a collector favorite since her lifespan, of just a few years, was so short. Skooter doll and her pal, Ricky doll, gave the younger set more representation.

Francie
(1966)

Bold splashy colors. Mini dresses with geometric shapes. Go-go boots. Heavily-mascaraed eyes. By the middle of the 1960s, an eruption of the attitude defined as "mod" had taken over music, makeup and fashion, so why not the toy world?

While Barbie doll fashions were concurrently changing with the times, Mattel introduced another Barbie family member who would fully embrace the meaning of mod.

In fact, Mattel even dubbed Francie "Barbie's 'MOD'ern cousin." Both straight-leg and bendable leg models were made, both with long, loose flipped hair. An added feature of the bendable leg dolls was rooted eyelashes, something Mattel also featured on Twist and Turn Barbie dolls of the same era.

Francie doll was a true chameleon, and there was rarely a look she couldn't pull off. Her fashions even had names reflecting the times: Gad-About, Leather Limelight, Swingin' Skimmy, Hip Knits and Fur-Out. You could almost hear the go-go music in the background.

left: *Go-go Francie doll! Check out those rooted eyelashes… Bendable Leg Francie, Barbie doll's cousin, could hold her own in the dance clubs.*

right: *Francie doll was available in straight leg — as well as a later bendable leg version, pictured at left.*

Francie

(straight leg)
Model #1140
Hair Colors: Blond, brunette
Current Value: **$400 MIB**

No Bangs Francie and Francie Twist and Turn

Model #1170
Hair Colors: Blond, brunette
Current Value: **$1,200 MIB** no bangs,
$500 MIB TNT

Hair Apparent:

Does a hairstyle really matter? Apparently to collectors it does. Around 1970, Francie doll's traditional hairstyle – long flippy hair with bangs – was altered on a doll that has come to be known as No Bangs Francie. This Twist and Turn doll, available in blond or brunette, featured a pulled-back hairstyle with no bangs. She's so rare, a Mint in Box example today could bring $1,200 or more. That's one expensive hairdo.

Rarity Alert:

Mattel's first African-American doll in the Barbie doll was her cousin Francie, now known in collectors' circles as Black Francie. The doll, with Twist and Turn body, featured several variations in hair and eye colors. She remains a rarity, commanding over $1,000 Mint in Box.

left: *"No Bangs" Francie is a valued collector favorite.*

right: *Known in collectors' circles as "Black Francie," this rare Twist and Turn doll can be worth big bucks in Mint condition.*

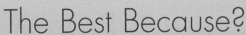

The Best Because?

In addition to ushering in the mod years, Francie added a multicultural element to the line. Just over a decade later, Black Barbie (1980) would be introduced.

Black Francie
Model #1100
Hair Colors: First issue: reddish, second issue: dark brown
Current Value: **$1,600 MIB** red hair, **$1,500 MIB** dark brown hair

Gay Parisienne
#964, 1959 (Pictured on a Ponytail #1.)
Current Value: **$4,000 MIP**

bestdressed

the great outfits

Even though the first Barbie doll was first introduced to buyers in a now-famous black-and-white swimsuit, it was obvious from that moment that Barbie doll was destined to become a fashion plate. Although her swimwear was utilitarian and far from trendy, she would soon wear outfits that embodied elegance, glamour, professionalism and an adventurous spirit.

Most early Barbie dolls donned the zebra-stripe swimsuit and were packaged in regular-issue boxes. Some of the earliest dolls, however, were found in "pink silhouette" boxes (a pale pink box with silhouetted figures of the dolls on the front). Early Ponytail dolls were dressed in outfits and placed in these boxes for store display only. Some of Barbie doll's most stylish (and now most valuable) outfits were modeled in these boxes.

Barbie doll's fashion catalog is epic and well-rounded. Here is a look at some of the best.

Strolling the Champs Elysee was never more fashionable than

note: *Prices in this section are for the outfit MIP, not including the doll.*

73

wearing *Gay Parisienne*, #964 (1959). The outfit is a rarity in itself, and the tiny items which have often been lost throughout the years (clutch purse, veiled hat) can command several hundred dollars each today.

Barbie doll also stylishly wore black with *Easter Parade*, #971 (1959). It is a classy black coat with vibrant apple-print sheath dress peeking out from underneath. Barbie doll's stylish bow hat is extremely hard to find today.

Since she had already visited Paris, Barbie doll's next European stop was Rome.

Made for only one year, *Roman Holiday*, #968 (1959), is crisp and fresh, just like Audrey Hepburn's memorable bike ride through the film of the same name. (Although there is no movie connection between the outfit's name and the film.)

All play and no work, however, wouldn't do. *Commuter Set*, #916 (1959-1960), is the epitome of working-girl class. Barbie doll dons proper white gloves and navy suit, and completes the look with a very "of the moment" frilly silk hat. The logo hatbox is a coveted piece from this set.

The *Busy Gal* #981 (1960-1961) ensemble is the perfect outfit for a luncheon meeting. Complete with sketch portfolio, Barbie doll is ready for her working lunch at *Vogue* or *Harper's Bazaar*.

When work was done, Barbie doll was ready to hit the open road in the appropriately-named *Open Road*, #985 (1961-1962) outfit. Practical traveling gear includes a safari-look coat (Anyone for the Outback?), but the cork wedge shoes would quickly put an end to too much hiking. Barbie

doll's tiny map is a coveted find; it was often lost on her travels. The map alone could bring $20 or more.

For an early touch of elegance, Barbie doll could turn to *Enchanted Evening*, #983 (1960-1963). It featured pink satin, faux fur, long gloves and pearls.

Just as classy too, is *Solo in the Spotlight*, #982 (1960-1964). This form-fitting shimmery black sheath turns Barbie doll into a songstress. She carries a pink chiffon scarf at the ready to fan the flames from swooning men in the audience.

One of the earliest store exclusive outfits was *Tickled Pink*, #1681, available from Sears in 1966. Its limited availability adds to its rarity and value today.

Simple enough for a stroll to the store or jaunt to a garden party, *Sheath Sensation*, #986 (1961-1964) is a solid hit. The clean simple lines of this red dress are accentuated with a straw hat and gloves.

Dressing up is always more fun with friends. Take, for example, *Friday Night Date*, #979 (1960-1964). If Sinatra and sodas were your plan, this jumper was perfect. Pair Barbie doll up with Allan doll dressed in *Sailor*, #796 (1963-1965) and she's ready for a whole new adventure! The outfit, which was actually designed for Ken doll, came complete with a U.S. Navy bag. All they needed was music to make the evening complete. Barbie doll in *Dancing Doll*, #1626 (1965) will do just fine, complete with tiny

right: The rare silk bow tie hat (hiding in the pocket of this photo) could bring $400 alone! Note that the Apple Print Sheath was released as its own dress (#917) in 1959-'60.

Easter Parade

#971, 1959 (Pictured on a Ponytail #3.)
Current Value: **$4,000 MIP**

record player and record (both are hard-to-find pieces).

But dates only last so long before work begins again. In 1966, Barbie doll was sent soaring as a *Pan American Airlines Stewardess*, #1678. After a previous stint at American Airlines, Barbie doll took flight and landed at this rival airlines. Made for only one year, this outfit remains one of the most coveted in the Barbie doll wardrobe.

While all these fashions are, in their own ways, lovely and important, few dresses are as important as Barbie doll's wedding dress. Dozens of styles have been created over the years, but it is her first dress that collectors recall and desire. *Wedding Day*, #972 (1959-1962) is a classic design. A wedding is generally considered a once-in-a-lifetime event, but Barbie doll's first wedding dress was one of many she would wear throughout the years. Ken doll's *Tuxedo*, #787 (1961-1965), on the other hand, served him well for many years until he sported the dapper *Here Comes the Groom* outfit in 1966. Ken doll's earliest formal wear includes a classic bow tie and cummerbund.

left: *Made for one year only, Roman Holiday is a crisp and fresh outfit.*
right: *Barbie doll shows off the best in office attire in Commuter Set.*

Roman Holiday
#968, 1959 (Pictured on a Ponytail #4.)
Current Value: **$4,800 MIP**

Commuter Set

#916, 1959-1960
Current Value: **$1,500 MIP**
REPRO ALERT: This exciting fashion was
reproduced in 1999 as part of Mattel's
Collectors' Request series.

right: *The hard-to-find portfolio under this Barbie doll's arm could bring $40 alone!*

Busy Gal
Current Value: **$400 MIP**
REPRO ALERT: Busy Gal was remade in 1995.

left: *Spotted these glasses? This rare pair could bring $100.*

right: *The map in jacket pocket was often lost, so today, one could bring $20.*

MATTEL ROAD MAP

Open Road
#985, 1961-1962
Current Value: **$350 MIP**

left: *An incredibly elegant outfit, Enchanted Evening showed that Barbie could dress for even the most formal occasions.*

Enchanted Evening

#983, 1960-1963 (Pictured on a Bubblecut Barbie.)
Current Value: **$385 MIP**
REPRO ALERT: This classic formal gown was offered on a collector doll in 1996.

left: *Torch songs were probably never hotter than when Barbie doll wore Solo in the Spotlight.*

Solo in the Spotlight

#982, 1960-1964 (Pictured on a Ponytail #4.)
Current Value: **$470 MIP**
REPRO ALERT: In 1995, this glamorous outfit was offered on both blond and brunette dolls.

81

right: *Tickled Pink was only available as a Sears exclusive, adding to its rarity and value on the collectors' market today.*

Tickled Pink

#1681, 1966 Sears Exclusive (Pictured on American Girl.)
Current Value: **$2,000 MIP**

Sheath Sensation

#986, 1961-1964 (Pictured on a Ponytail #3.)
Current Value: **$150 MIP**

Friday Night Date

#979, 1960-1964
Current Value: **$245 MIP**

Sailor

#796, 1963-1965 (Pictured on Allan.)
Current Value: **$120 MIP**

Dancing Doll

#1626, 1965
Current Value: **$450 MIP**

left: *All around, this is a rare outfit, but the logo hat is extremely hard to find.*

Pan American Airlines
Stewardess

#1678, 1966 (Pictured on American Girl.)
Current Value: **$4,000 MIP**

this spread: *A classic scene — Barbie doll in Wedding Day and Ken doll in his tux.*

Wedding Day

#972, 1959-1962
Current Value: **$385 MIP**
REPRO ALERT: The Wedding Day outfit was
made as a reproduction in 1997.

Tuxedo

#787, 1961-1965
Current Value: **$245 MIP**

Talking Busy Steffie
Model #1186
Hair Colors: Blond
Current Value: **$350 MIB**

word of the decade: action

After an era of change, Barbie doll wasn't ready to stagnate. Becoming more popular than ever, she was moving beyond being a fashion doll, and was changing with the beat of the 1970s, which would truly be Barbie doll's era of "action."

Mattel's plan for the decade appeared, on the surface, somewhat gimmicky. In the decade's earliest dolls, Mattel strived to bring Barbie doll and her friends to life with technology designed to make the dolls "move." While the Live Action dolls could dance on a stand, Busy Barbie could grab things with her newly-designed hands and Walk Lively Barbie could strut her stuff. Moving bodies, growing hair and a kissing mechanism were some additional actions Mattel dreamed up for the dolls for the 1970s.

While these innovations were appropriate for the time, somehow they differed greatly from the classic changes of the 1960s — the more subtle, yet enduring, alterations in the doll's image.

left: *Talking Busy Steffie epitomized the new spirit of "dolls that do things" at Mattel, whether it was talking, walking or carrying accessories.*
right: *She's groovin'… with a special stand, this hip Live Action Barbie could dance to the music.*

But today, the 1970s dolls are finally being considered collectible. Collectors remembering this era avidly seek these dolls, even if the doll's "actions" have long been worn out.

The mechanical gimmicks of the 1970s had worn out their welcome, and by the 1980s, Mattel shifted gears once again to enter a decade of culture. Barbie doll would go on to embrace more of her audience in the 1980s — the global audience.

Live Action Barbie (1970)

With the Age of Aquarius dawning, Barbie doll needed to be ready in a psychedelic swirled get-up, adorned

left: *The Dawning of the Age of Live-Action Barbie — a 1970 debut that soon spawned a slew of "Live Action" friends.*
following spread: *Here they are — the Live Action Gang — P.J., Christie, Ken and Barbie.*

with faux suede fringe.

The 1970s were definitely in full swing, at least where this doll was concerned. Like her Dramatic New Living counterpart, Live Action Barbie was movin' and groovin'. Thanks to a special stand, Live Action Barbie could "dance to your favorite music." One touch of the "touch and go" stand set off a whirling dervish of frantic dancing.

Do Like I Do:

Live Action Barbie doll's box touted her moves — "I dance to your favorite music," "I dance more than ever before," "Start the action, touch my touch n' go stand," and "There's lots I do — just like you."

The Best Because?

Hippie chic had arrived, reflected in Barbie doll's attitude, body, hair and fashions. Soon, the entire gang of Barbie doll's friends would go "Live Action."

Live Action P.J.
Model #1156
Hair Colors: Blond
Current Value: **$250 MIB**

Live Action Christie
Model #1175
Hair Colors: Black
Current Value: **$250 MIB**

Live Action Barbie

Model #1155
Hair Colors: Blond
Current Value: **$150 MIB**

Live Action Ken

Model #1159
Hair Colors: Painted brown
Current Value: **$150 MIB**

Dramatic New
Living Barbie

Model #1116
Hair Colors: Blond, brunette
Current Value: **$275 MIB**

Dramatic New Living Barbie
(1970)

A veritable earthquake of activity shook up the Barbie dolls Mattel introduced at the turn of the decade. Dramatic New Living Barbie arrived in 1970, and if you didn't notice her futuristic silver and gold lamé swimsuit, you couldn't miss the doll's new attitude.

While Twist and Turn was an important innovation for its time, it was elementary compared to the range of motion of Dramatic New Living Barbie. TNT could twist, but this doll could move.

Fully poseable, Dramatic New Living Barbie featured bendable legs, twisting waist (all the better to shimmy with), bendable elbows and wrists (to strike those disco poses), a rotating head and loose leg and arm sockets (cheerleader splits were no problem!). She sits! She bends! She moves just like you (well, maybe if you were double-jointed).

Dramatic face paint and rooted eyelashes added to the glam. Even under that orange mesh cover-up, it was obvious this doll was something special.

left: *The culmination of all Barbie dolls up to this point—Dramatic New Living Barbie was the first fully poseable model. She could even do the splits!*
right: *Dramatic New Living Barbie featured a strangely sci-fi wardrobe. And just look at those lashes!*

The Best Because?

This doll literally shook up the Barbie doll line. Poseability increased play value, moving Barbie doll into the 1970s.

95

Barbie with Growin' Pretty Hair
(1971)

This doll featured hair that could be lengthened or shortened at will – well, not exactly that easily, but with a mild tug. Barbie doll's retractable ponytail embraced the hair play craze; she even came with hairpieces and accessories to complete the look.

Great fun and utility . . . if used correctly. Sometimes aspiring hairstylists did more than just crimp and curl hair. Often, this doll's lifespan was, ahem, cut short with a swift snip of the scissors.

The Best Because?

It made a lot more sense to offer a doll with lots of hairdo possibilities, rather than the somewhat surrealistic Hair Fair Barbie issued at the same time. Hair Fair Barbie wasn't a doll at all, just a head sold in a set with wigs and accessories.

left: *A light tug, some curlers and… pouf! A whole new Barbie doll. Just make sure not to pull too hard or trim too much off the top.*

right: *Another new Barbie doll with an added feature—Growin' Pretty Hair. The doll was issued in 1972 with a patterned skirt.*

Barbie with Growin' Pretty Hair

(First Issue, pink dress)
Model #1144
Hair Colors: Blond
Current Value: **$300 MIB**

Walk Lively Barbie

Model #1182
Hair Colors: Blond
Current Value: **$225 MIB**

Walk Lively Barbie
(1971)

Nancy Sinatra had nothing on this fancy strutter. Even though Walk Lively Barbie wore pilgrim shoes, not white go-go boots, she could walk smoothly (and swing her arms accordingly) on a special stand.

The Best Because?

Mattel was continually progressing in making Barbie doll more mobile. This doll renewed that trend.

left: *Literally, made for walkin'… Walk Lively Barbie, debuting in 1971, was packaged with a special stand that allowed her to walk and swing her arms, too.*

barbie trivia

A Willowy Blond
Having sported the tan-kissed skin of Malibu, Barbie might appear to be a true California girl. Actually, according to Mattel lore, Barbie hails from the fictional Willows, Wisconsin.

99

Malibu Barbie
(The Sun Set)
(1971)

Who can forget her blissfully tan skin? Her blue-eyed, blond-hair surfer girl look? Her curvaceous body?

Malibu Barbie was one of the earliest dolls to hit the essence of little girls' play patterns. Sure, hair play was hot, but taking Barbie doll to the beach or the pool was just plain cool.

The Best Because?

The Malibu look made such a splash it was used on just about every Barbie doll friend. It also spawned a number of licensed products, like Colorforms sets, paper dolls and coloring books. Almost continually since her introduction, variations of Malibu Barbie have been eagerly snatched up.

left: *Malibu Barbie really established a look that first springs to mind, even today, when someone says "Barbie."*
right*: Malibu Barbie, 1971, was so instantly popular that virtually every Barbie doll friend became "Malibu-ized" before too long.*

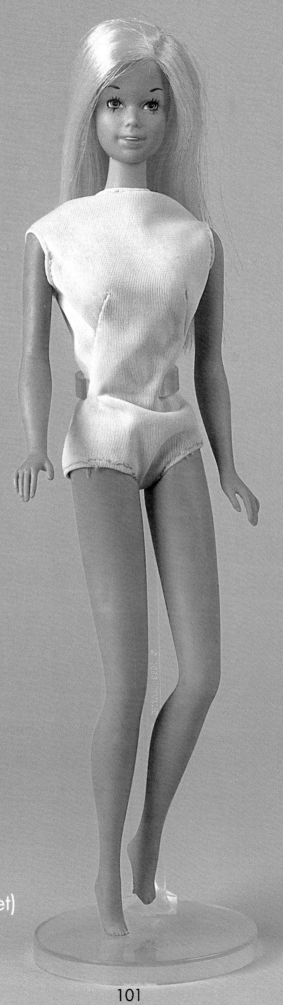

Malibu Barbie
(first issue, The Sun Set)

Model #1067
Hair Colors: Blond
Current Value: **$60 MIB**

Busy Barbie

Model #3311
Hair Colors: Blond
Current Value: **$300 MIB**

Busy
Barbie
(1971)

Busy Barbie, while delicate, featured working hands. While the innovations on this doll were designed to make Barbie doll more active and powerful ("gripping" hands, TNT waist), they ultimately didn't last long. Production costs were prohibitive, and the dolls' joints a bit too fragile to survive a lot of play.

left: *Introduced with gripping hands in 1971, Busy Barbie could bring accessories along even easier.*
below: *A close-up view of the new "Busy Hands." They're really quite mechanical-looking.*

The Best
Because?

Busy Barbie, like the other motion-packed dolls before her, was awash in a sea of gimmicks Mattel had been using quite often during this time. Busy Barbie was innovative . . . and boy, could she hail a cab.

Busy Ken
Model #3314
Hair Colors: Painted brown
Current Value: **$165 MIB**

Talking Busy Barbie

Model #1195
Hair Colors: Blond
Current Value: **$300 MIB**

Busy Steffie

Model #3312
Hair Colors: Brunette
Current Value: **$350 MIB**

Busy Francie
Model #3313
Hair Colors: Blond
Current Value: **$425 MIB**

this spread: *Keepin' busy! Pictured left to right are: Talking Busy Steffie, Busy Steffie, Busy Ken, Busy Barbie, Busy Francie and Talking Busy Barbie.*

Quick Curl Barbie

Model #4220
Hair Colors: Blond
Current Value: **$80 MIB**

Quick Curl Barbie
(1972)

Basic hair play took on an added dimension with Quick Curl Barbie. Now this very demure doll featured hair that really curled, thanks to the included curler, comb and brush.

The Best Because?

A classic addition to continuing line of "gimmicky" dolls of the 1970s.

left: *Again, with the hair… Quick Curl Barbie, introduced in 1972, had hair that really curled.*

right: *Aspiring hairdressers could count on one more Barbie for practice.*

below*: Another set of those small, easy-to-lose accessories, curlers.*

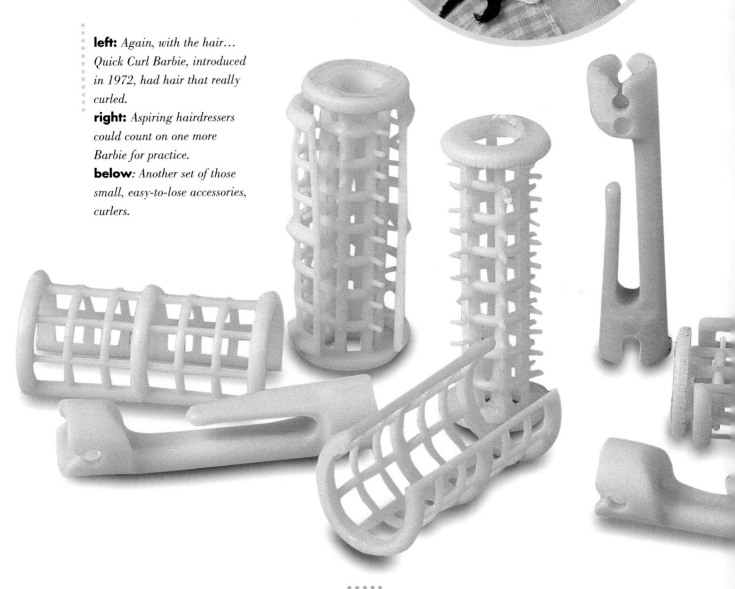

Montgomery Ward Barbie
(1972)

In one of the first "reissues" of sorts, Mattel created a reproduction of an early brunette Ponytail to commemorate the 100th anniversary of Montgomery Ward stores. Dressed in the familiar black and white swimsuit, the doll was sold in stores in a sparse pink box under the name "The Original Barbie." Dolls ordered through the catalog were shipped in plain boxes.

right: *In a first reissue, the Montgomery Ward 100th Anniversary Barbie was sold in a plain pink box and featured the doll in the black and white swimsuit of days gone by.*

The Best Because?

The age of reproductions and store exclusives had begun, something that would continue throughout Barbie doll history.

Montgomery
Ward 100th
Anniversary
Barbie

Model #3210
Hair Colors: Brunette
Current Value: **$800 MIB**

Mod Hair Ken

Model #4224
Hair Colors: Brunette
Current Value: **$65 MIB**

Mod Hair Ken
(1972)

Mod Hair Ken was his first appearance with rooted hair since his early 1960s fuzzy head days.

Wrapped up in the grooviness of the 1970s, Mattel topped this doll (dressed in brown buffalo-checked jacket and white dickey) with a fairly choppy do.

But wait, there's more! Mod Hair Ken came complete with a sheet of brown flocked accoutrements like beard, mustache and sideburns. Just the thing when you needed a disguise.

Now and Then:

Mod Hair Ken doll's '70s look would only be surpassed by 1975's Now Look Ken. The long hair look was in, even for men, and Ken doll sported side-parted shoulder length hair. Apparently the tan leisure suit wasn't enough; this Ken doll also donned a breezy turquoise scarf.

The Best Because?

The times were changing, and Mattel was proving it change with them. With Barbie doll, it was easier to dress her up and change her hairdo; with an already good-looking guy like Ken doll, modernizing him was more challenging. In later years, Mattel wavered between molded hair and rooted hair dolls.

left: *Ken doll at the height of 1970s fashion.*
right: *Arriving in 1972, he was the first rooted-hair Ken to come along in about 10 years. In keeping with the zeitgeist, Mod Hair Ken could even be decked out in a flocked beard, mustache and sideburns.*

Free Moving Barbie
(1974)

This mid-1970s doll fully embraced Mattel's move toward motion. With a little help from her friends (and a lever on her back), Barbie doll could swing her arms and move her upper torso.

The Best Because?

The Free Moving mechanism was yet another innovation meant to create new play scenarios for Barbie. A good idea, but this doll had a short lifespan.

right: *With a little help from a lever, this Free Moving Barbie could really swing.*
below: *Naturally, once a Free Moving Barbie arrived in 1974, a similar Ken doll followed.*

Free Moving Barbie

Model #7270
Hair Colors: Blond
Current Value: **$100 MIB**

Sweet 16
(1974)

Never been kissed? Although Barbie doll had only been around 15 years, Mattel jumped the gun on this special birthday and introduced this fairly inexpensive carded doll in 1974. This aptly-named doll attempted to reach a younger, eager-to-reach-their-teen-years audience that still played with toys.

The Best Because?

Her prim pink look was a priceless reminder of the innocence of turning sweet 16. Her accessories—including scented sticker barrettes—perfectly embraced the budding vanity of her audience.

Kissing Barbie
(1979)

In a decade of dolls that walked, talked, danced and shimmied, Mattel put its money where Barbie doll's mouth was. All she had to do was gloss (lipstick included), pucker and SWAK! (A mechanism on the doll's back, when pushed, triggered the pucker motion and sound.)

left: *In 1979, Kissing Barbie started smoochin' the day away. This was the true frontier in action-oriented Barbies.*
right: *Released in 1974, Sweet 16 was pushed a bit early—Barbie doll was really introduced in 1959, fifteen years earlier.*

Kissing Barbie
Model #2597
Hair Colors: Blond
Current Value: **$65 MIB**

The Best Because?

Aside from the perpetual fish-lips look, this doll pushed the limit of gimmicks.

Sweet 16

Model #7796
Hair Colors: Blond
Current Value: **$125 MIB**

Supersize Barbie
(1977)

It might work for french fries, but Supersize Barbie may have been too much of a good thing. It was the experiment that just never caught on.

It's uncertain what the motivation was to turn Barbie doll into an Amazon (at 18 inches, she towered over her 11-1/2-inch cohorts). Trouble was, Supersize Barbie couldn't share her friends' clothes, didn't fit into their houses and wouldn't feel comfortable at a slumber party.

The Best Because?

Another testament to innovation in the 1970s, this test didn't work. But it did open the door to much later trials that may have fared better, such as the mid-1990s My Size Barbie. At 3-feet tall, this doll was better poised for success since it could wear its owner's clothes.

right: *There was no way these two were sharing outfits.*
far right: *Way taller than the Ken doll, Supersize Barbie measured in at 18 inches.*

Supersize Barbie
Model #9828
Hair Colors: Blond
Current Value: **$200 MIB**

Superstar Barbie

Model #9720
Hair Colors: Blond
Current Value: **$70 MIB**

Superstar Barbie
(1977)

It was the late 1970s. Disco balls were in full swing; dance garb was electric, brassy, even garish. It was a feel-good era of style and sound, and Barbie doll was ready to pump up the volume.

After almost 20 years and dozens of reincarnations, Barbie doll put her best face forward — she was going to be a Superstar! The Superstar face was decidedly different from the stoic visages of Barbie doll's early years. Glamour was the watchword, and Barbie doll's new wide-eyed, smiling face was ready for anything.

left: *Barbie doll's face underwent a major style change with Superstar Barbie, released in 1977.*
right: *Larger eyes and more widely-set cheekbones mark the difference in Superstar Barbie.*

The Best Because?

Decked out in glittery wrap and jewelry, Superstar Barbie debuted one of the most famous faces America's favorite doll would ever sport. It was a fresh — and longterm — look.

Stars 'n Stripes Collection,
Navy Barbie

Model #9694
Hair Color: Black
Current Value: **$35 MIB**

bestgigs
chapterfour

careers through the years

N aturally, Barbie doll's early work life matched the career trajectories of the times. At first billed as a "teen-age fashion model," she soon found herself working as a nurse, student teacher, ballerina or fashion model. The fact is, Mattel was deeply in tune with the spirit of the times whenever they created a new identity or opportunity for the Barbie doll.

left: *In 1991, Mattel released Stars 'n Stripes Navy Barbie — one of many military-inspired dolls that came about in the 1990s.*
right: *Midge doll was at work, too. The Registered Nurse outfit included glasses, a hot water bottle and a diploma.*
bottom: *An almost fashion-plate look at the world of nursing from the Barbie doll catalog, early 1960s.*

#991

REGISTERED NURSE
(without doll) #991
Barbie cures patients in a trim white cotton uniform with zipper back, buttoned blouse and real hip pockets. With her spectacles and graduate nurse's cap, she wears a navy blue cape khaki in red silk for outside calls. Hot water bottle, diploma, medicine bottle and spoon complete the set. $5.00

Registered Nurse
(Fashion seen on Midge.)

Even back in the early 1960s, Barbie doll was exploring new careers that were not necessarily considered "women's work" at the time. Consider the 1964 Miss Astronaut suit, which came at a peak time in the U.S. space program. It was still a few years before *man* landed on the moon, but Barbie doll was already suited up.

Barbie doll has had her share of "best gigs" in more than 40 years. Most recently, she's become a superhero (Wonder Woman), NASCAR driver, paleontologist and even run for president of the United States.

The images in this section are just a sampling of some of Barbie doll's best occupations through the years. They've all been pretty exciting.

left: *It seems that Ken doll would follow Barbie doll (or in this case, Midge doll) just about anywhere — even into orbit!*

right: *The 1964 Miss Astronaut suit predated American women's role in NASA by many years. It's interesting to see the new career opportunities open up for Barbie doll as the space program picked up steam. The helmet Midge doll wears is not original, however, but created for the photo.*

right: *In a return to more down-to-earth work, Mattel introduced the Barbie Student Teacher outfit.*

right: *Great work if you can get it—Quick Curl Miss America. A natural step for a doll once billed as a "teenage fashion model," even though she'd already explored a variety of careers.*

Quick Curl Miss America
Model #8697
Hair Color: Blond
Current Value: **$75 MIB**

right: *Not officially part of the Stars 'n Stripes series, American Beauties Army Barbie appeared in 1989.*

American Beauties
Army Barbie

Model #3966
Hair Color: Blond
Current Value: **$40 MIB**

left: An official Stars 'n Stripes release, Air Force Barbie. The doll's pilot garb, as opposed to a dress uniform, reflects the changing roles for women in the military.

Stars 'n Stripes Collection, Air Force Barbie

Model #3360
Hair Color: Blond
Current Value: **$50 MIB**

right: *When the Toys R Us Police Officer Barbie was released in 1993, the idea of a female police officer working a beat didn't even raise an eyebrow.*

Police Officer Barbie,
Toys R Us exclusive
Model #10689
Hair Color: Black
Current Value: **$65 MIB**

left: *Another Toys R Us exclusive, Firefighter Barbie was another doll engaged in dangerous work. At least she had a cute companion to help out.*

Firefighter Barbie,
Toys R Us exclusive

Model #13553
Hair Color: Blond
Current Value: **$25 MIB**

Stars 'n Stripes
Army Ken

this spread: *Ready for inspection.*
A sampling of military-themed dolls
including the 1992 Stars 'n Stripes
Rendezvous with Destiny Barbie and Ken.

Model #5619
Hair Color: Black
Current Value: **$30 MIB**

Stars 'n Stripes
Army Barbie

Stars 'n Stripes
Marine Corps Barbie

Stars 'n Stripes
Marine Corps Ken

Model #1234
Hair Color: Blond
Current Value: **$40 MIB**

Model #7594
Hair Color: Black
Current Value: **$35 MIB**

Model #5352
Hair Color: Painted Brown
Current Value: **$40 MIB**

Dolls of the World

Japanese Barbie
Model #9481
Hair Color: Black
Current Value: **$125 MIB**

1980s
chapterfive

word of the decade: culture

In the same way that Mattel set a trend with the introduction of the Barbie doll in 1959, it would continue to do so with the releases in the 1980s.

The 1980s was a decade in which ethnic walls would crumble with the introduction of the International series, which placed Barbie dolls in the authentic garb of far-flung nations. And although she started with Europe, she eventually traveled to all continents.

The International series and the later Happy Holidays line eventually ushered in the 1990s, which would truly be Barbie doll's coming of age as a collectible. Nothing that had come before would rival Mattel's efforts in pleasing a new generation of audience — the adult collector.

left: *Dolls taking on a decidedly international flair were introduced in the 1980s. The Japanese Barbie shown here arrived on the scene in 1985.*

Black Barbie

Model #1293
Hair Colors: Black
Current Value: **$100 MIB**

Black Barbie
(1980)

Mattel forayed into the multicultural domain about a decade before the introduction of Black Barbie with the introduction of Black Francie, Barbie doll's cousin. Barbie doll's African-American friend, Christie, also appeared in the late 1960s.

Based on the Twist and Turn doll, Black Barbie, as described on her box, was "black, beautiful and dynamite." She featured a bold, stylish red gown with gold accents and tailored afro hair.

All in the Family:

A notable inclusion to Mattel's multicultural family was Julia, based on the Diahann Carroll television series. Introduced in 1969, the African-American doll came dressed (among other outfits) as a nurse. Today, this celebrity doll is valued at $200 or more in Mint in Box condition.

left: *In 1980, Mattel released the first black Barbie doll.* **right:** *Black Barbie was described on Mattel's packaging as "black, beautiful and dynamite."*

The Best Because:

This was a watershed moment for Mattel. In embracing other cultures, Mattel firmly established Barbie doll for everyone, and for the rest of her history, the doll has been available in Caucasian and African-American versions, as well as other ethnicities.

Hispanic Barbie
(1980)

To meet the demands of a growing ethnic market, Mattel's first Black and Hispanic Barbie dolls were released concurrently. This doll was released primarily in Spanish-speaking markets.

The Best Because:

Adjustments in face molds and dress led the way for Mattel's soon-to-follow International series.

left: *You could see the beginnings of the International Series with the release of the black and Hispanic Barbie dolls.*
right: *Hola! Hispanic Barbie was another new release for Mattel in 1980.*

Hispanic Barbie
Model #1292
Hair Colors: Black
Current Value: **$75 MIB**

Dream Date Barbie
Model #5868
Hair Colors: Blond
Current Value: **$25 MIB**

Dream Date Barbie
(1983)

You can easily picture Dream Date Barbie hailing a cab as easily as waving from the window of her limo. And why not? This go-getter epitomized Barbie doll's 1980s look. A Superstar face surrounded by cascades of blond — that was the fresh, healthy glow the 1980s dolls sported. And the word in 1980s fashion was "excess." With a sequined top and satin skirt, this Barbie doll was, indeed, a dream date.

The Best Because?

While Malibu Barbie represented the 1970s, Dream Date Barbie was just one of many similar-looking 1980s dolls. Painted faces and clothes may have changed, but underneath it all, the Superstar mold and TNT body remained a standard for more than 10 years.

left: *Dream Date Barbie featured the doe-eyed look and voluminous hair that epitomized the decade.*
right: *Some of Dream Date Barbie doll's flashy sequins. Definitely a sign of glamorous times.*

Western Barbie

Model #1757
Hair Colors: Two-tone blond
Current Value: **$40 MIB**

Western Barbie
(1980)

Hey, cowboy! Wanna go to the rodeo? Wink, wink.

Capitalizing on the trendy Western craze, Mattel released Western Barbie. While the Western concept (and her jazzy jumpsuit) was well-conceived, Mattel's decision to make the doll wink was just a little confusing.

Why was she winking? At whom? Did she have a secret?

This wasn't one of the most attractive face molds in Barbie doll history, and it was never used again. (Remarkably, though, workable winkers aren't too hard to come by today.)

The Best Because:

Hard to say, but she was just so unique she had to be included. She is a treat to find at the bottom of a pile of rummage sale dolls, but she still looks somewhat offbeat staring up at you.

far left: *A button on her back made Western Barbie wink, "Howdy, Pardner!"*
left: *All gussied up for the dude ranch — Western Ken.*
following spread: *Yup, they're headin' out for a ride, Western Skipper, Barbie and Ken dolls.*

Western Skipper
Model #5029
Hair Color: Blond
Current Value: **$30 MIB**

Western Barbie
Model #1757
Hair Color: Blond
Current Value: **$40 MIB**

Western Ken
Model #3600
Hair Color: Painted brown
Current Value: **$40 MIB**

Happy Holidays Series
(1988-1998)

In the late 1980s, it was unthinkable…possibly even to Mattel…that anyone would pay more than $10 for a Barbie doll. However, the first series of dolls aimed specifically at collectors debuted in 1988 with the Happy Holiday Series.

Happy Holidays #1, 1988

Model #1703
Hair Colors: Blond
Current Value: **$700 MIB**

Happy Holidays #2, 1989

Model #3253
Hair Colors: Blond
Current Value: **$175 MIB**

Happy Holidays #3, 1990

Black doll, black hair, Model #4543 **$85 MIB**
White doll, blond hair, Model #4098 **$110 MIB**

The high-quality doll and packaging raised the price to $19.99. The good news was that the doll was an instant success, surpassing perhaps even Mattel's wildest dreams.

Happy Holidays #5, 1992

Black doll, black hair, Model #2396 **$80 MIB**
White doll, blond hair, Model #1429 **$120 MIB**

Happy Holidays #4, 1991

Black doll, black hair, Model #2696 **$100 MIB**
White doll, blond hair, Model #1871 **$150 MIB**

Happy Holidays #6, 1993

Black doll, black hair, Model #10911 **$60 MIB**
White doll, blond hair, Model #10824 **$95 MIB**

Happy Holidays #7, 1994

Black doll, black hair, Model #12156 **$75 MIB**
White doll, blond hair, Model #12155 **$120 MIB**
*Note: The brunette doll pictured is a special 35th anniversary
doll, sold exclusively at Walt Disney World. Exclusives can
command higher aftermarket prices.*

Happy Holidays #8, 1995

Black doll, black hair, Model #14124 **$55 MIB**
White doll, blond hair, Model #14123 **$65 MIB**

Happy Holidays #9, 1996

Black doll, black hair, Model #15647
White doll, brunette hair, Model #15646
Current Value: **$55 MIB for each**
*Note: The brunette doll was available via mass market.
The blonde was a Barbie Collector's Club exclusive. These
collector's editions can command higher aftermarket prices.*

Happy Holidays #10, 1997

Black doll, black hair, Model #17833
White doll, blond hair, Model #17832
Current Value: **$25 MIB for each**

Supply & Demand

Mattel learned an important collecting lesson with this series – the fine line between satisfying consumer demand and satisfying collector demand. Consumers want dolls to be readily available. Likewise, while collectors want the dolls just as avidly, too many dolls dash collector value.

High demand (and short supply) for the first Happy Holidays doll caused Mattel to steadily increase the number of dolls produced each year. Eventually, a glut occurred, leaving dazzling dolls languishing on store shelves long after the holiday season.

Low production numbers and high demand are directly responsible for the first Happy Holidays doll's current secondary market value — about $700 or more.

The Best Because?

Happy Holidays, not originally intended as a continuing series, became one of the longest-lasting and most successful series, lasting until 1998. It directly influenced the era of higher-end collectible dolls, opening the door to dolls that crashed through the retail price ceiling. Due to the acceptance of Happy Holidays, consumers seemed ready to embrace higher prices for higher-quality collectible dolls.

Happy Holidays #11, 1998

Black doll, black hair, Model #20201
White doll, blond hair, Model #20200
Current Value: **$25 MIB for each**

Irish Barbie
Model #7517
Hair Color: Reddish brown
Current Value: **$115 MIB**

International Series/ Dolls of the World
(1980-present)

By 1980, Barbie doll was already well-versed in fashion and society, and had been well-travelled through the fashions she donned. The 1965 fashion Aboard Ship offered her the world by sea. As a Pan Am stewardess in 1966, she skytrotted to places unknown. And the early 1960s Ski Queen swooshed down the slopes in Aspen and Vail.

But no longer content to be just a visitor, the ethnically-ambiguous Barbie doll would break free and cross barriers previously untested.

She would become a citizen of the globe through the International series, one of Mattel's earliest official Barbie doll "series."

Cheerio! Ciao! Bonjour! Europe was first on Barbie doll's ticket to ride—the first three countries Barbie doll would pay tribute to were England, Italy and France. While many children and adults

The Best Because?

The Dolls of the World are history personified. They effortlessly transport Barbie doll to far-flung places some children and adults could only dream about visiting. Their fashions and accessories relay the customs and culture of other lands, helping embrace other ethnicities.

already considered Barbie doll a queen, the first doll in the series, Royal Barbie, featured Barbie doll as a British royal. With tiara and sash, she could have been mistaken as a Miss America contestant.

Italian Barbie, dressed in peasant blouse, featured a unique head mold. And ooh la la, Parisian Barbie (which utilized the Steffie head mold) was the stereotypical can-can dancer.

Several of the earlier dolls were reissued with new faces and attire, and after a few years, Mattel renamed the line "Dolls of the World." The series, still active in 2000, has targeted all corners of the globe; all seven continents have been represented.

barbie trivia
From Paris to Peru
Think Barbie is just an American phenomenon? You don't get to be such a classic without traveling the globe. She may be America's favorite doll, but Barbie is sold in more than 140 countries across the world. She was first introduced to Europe in 1961.

left: *Not the first in the International Series, but one of the most valuable—Irish Barbie, 1984.*

following left page: *Also debuting in 1980, Italian Barbie. Mattel's interest in ethnic dolls was definitely piqued considering the release of black, Hispanic, Royal and Italian Barbie all occurred in the same year.*

following right page: *Considered the first of the bunch the English or Royal Barbie was introduced in 1980.*

Italian Barbie

Model #1601
Hair Color: Brunette
Current Value: **$50 MIB**

Royal Barbie
Model #1601
Hair Color: Blond
Current Value: **$175 MIB**

this spread: *An International gathering,
from left to right: Nigerian, Italian, Royal ,
Parisian (first issue, seated) Japanese,
Kenyan and Irish Barbie dolls.*

Sunsational Malibu Ken, black

Model #3849
Hair Color: Black afro
Current Value: **$35 MIB**

Sunsational Malibu Ken
(1981)

Black Barbie had just debuted, so naturally, a black Ken doll should follow. Sporting a trendy Afro, the first black Ken doll was all set for a day at the beach in swim trunks and shades.

Part of the Malibu family, Sunsational Malibu Ken had a white counterpart (with molded blond hair). Although Mattel never made a black Sunsational Malibu Barbie, they created many versions of Barbie doll's black friend, Christie (including a swimsuit-clad Malibu version).

The Best Because?

The first black Ken doll broke the color barrier for the male dolls line.

left: *In 1981, one year after the launch of the first black Barbie, Sunsational Malibu Ken, the first black Ken, appeared.*
right: *Accessories like the sunglasses shown here just made the dolls even more fun.*

below: *Rocker Ken, the ideal counterpart to Rocker Barbie.*
right: *Rocker Barbie #2 and Ken, mid-1980s, epitomized the MTV era.*

Rocker Barbie
(1986)

In the 1980s, girls were jamming to hair bands like Poison and Quiet Riot. But Barbie doll could lead a band of her own—accordingly dubbed "The Rockers."

According to Mattel's 1985 annual report, "Times change and so does the Barbie doll. Her ability to keep up-to-date is a key to her continuing success. Girls today can become anything they want to be, from a glamorous personality to astronaut to rock star, just like Barbie. . ."

Created from the spirit of that report was Mattel's new advertising slogan — "We girls can do anything, right, Barbie?"

Not only did Barbie doll have the beat, she had the baubles to go with it. Her MTV look was in line with her contemporaries (the Go Gos or a toned-down Madonna come to mind). Pink, purple, glitz, glam, gobs of eye shadow and "big hair" really rocked.

So popular was this persona that Mattel issued a second Rocker Barbie (with daring midriff-baring top and silver pants) the following year. And she was, of course, joined by Rocker Ken.

The Best Because?

In becoming a rock star, Barbie doll embraced the "do anything" tone set by the dolls in produced in the 1980s and later.

Rocker Barbie #2
Model #3055
Hair Color: Blond
Current Value: **$25 MIB**

Rocker Ken
Model #3131
Hair Color: Blond
Current Value: **$30 MIB**

bestbanter

controversial dolls

Being the queen of fashion dolls is quite a distinction, and Barbie doll has worn her badge honorably for more than 40 years.

But the road hasn't always been paved with satin and lace. In fact, Mattel's Barbie doll has been the much-talked-about subject of many a controversy.

It hasn't really hurt any, though. If anything, controversy has only fueled collectors' interest. As it happens, there have been several times in the doll's history that have given pause to parents and collectors alike.

Here's a look at four of the most talked-about dolls.

left: *Growing up Skipper, released in 1977.*
right: *Earring Magic Ken, a controversial doll from 1993.*

Teen Talk Barbie

Model #5745
Hair colors: blond, brunette
Current Value: **$275 MIB** ("Math class"
variation) **$45 MIB** (for other variations).

Teen Talk Barbie
(1992)

When Teen Talk Barbie uttered the phrase "Math class is tough" upon release in 1992, women's groups argued that it evoked a negative image. While that was up for debate at the time, it has added up to major popularity on the secondary market ever since.

The Best Because?

By the 1990s, talking dolls were nothing new, but they are always a favorite, even when phrases the dolls utter were considerably different from the earlier talk of dancing and dating.

left: *Teen Talk Barbie, like many of us, struggled with math.*

165

Earring Magic Ken
(1993)

Trendiness was the goal, but Earring Magic Ken doll's fashion was greatly misinterpreted at the time of release. However, Earring Magic Ken sold out quickly, and his aftermarket value continues to climb.

The Best Because?

Earring Magic Ken has become one of the most memorable male dolls in history, due to questions about his costuming.

left: *This was the first time Ken sported an earring, but it wouldn't be the last.*
right: *Earring Magic Ken was released in 1993.*

Earring Magic Ken
Model #2290
Hair colors: Painted with blond streaks
Current Value: **$45 MIB**

Growing Up Skipper

Model #7259
Hair colors: Blond
Current Value: **$80 MIB**

Growing Up Skipper
(1977)

The proportionate size of Barbie doll's bust has always been questioned. However, when Growing Up Skipper was released, a mere twist of her shoulders made her bustline skip a few cup sizes. Skipper doll's friend, Ginger, also came in a Growing Up variety.

The Best Because?

Playing with this doll had to be better than watching health room videos about "coming of age." Anatomically-morphing dolls have never quite taken hold on store shelves, and they always incite controversy. While Growing Up Skipper and Ginger are a testament to Mattel's innovative prowess, the "growing up" experimenting ended with these dolls.

left: *Growing Up Skipper was a way that Mattel tried making the dolls more lifelike. Possibly as a way of appealing to girls who were just beginning to feel too old to play with dolls.*

right: *Skipper transformed easily through adolescence.*

Teacher Barbie
(1995)

The hubbub here wasn't a concern over Barbie doll's choice of career but rather her wardrobe. The first release of Teacher Barbie included a doll wearing a cleverly-designed jumper, but no underwear. Mattel remedied the situation, not with cloth but painted-on underwear.

The Best Because?

When the public starts talking about a doll's undergarments, you know it must be a slow news day. The controversy over this doll was probably lost on most buyers, and aside from the lack of underclothing (don't kids take doll's clothes off anyway?), Teacher Barbie still managed to be a commanding presence in the classroom.

right: *Teacher Barbie, a 1995 release.*

Teacher Barbie

Model #13914
Hair colors: Blond
Current Value: **$50 MIB**

Classic Ballet, Marzipan Barbie

Model #20581
Hair Color: Blond
Current Value: **$30 MIB**

1990s

word of the decade: collectible

By the 1990s, no longer were little girls the only viable market for Barbie dolls. Adult collectors were making up an increasingly larger audience, one that was willing to pay top dollar for higher-quality dolls. Collectibility had become the keyword, and that distinct tenet was evident in the some of the new dolls Mattel brought to the marketplace in that era. Of paramount import to collectors, Mattel realized, were quality and edition size. Recognizing this, the company focused on special series, store exclusives and gift sets designed to entice collectors. The Bob Mackie series, especially, is an example of how higher-end dolls (often more than $100) have thrived in a collector climate, both on the retail and secondary markets.

There are limitations, Mattel has learned, on what collectors will support. The 1995 introduction of the Pink Splendor doll, which retailed for $900, tested the price limit, and the 1996 Star Trek gift set was, perhaps, overproduced. It ended up on clearance racks at seriously slashed prices.

But still, some 40+ years after making her grand entrance, who would have thought that adults would be one of the primary audiences for Barbie dolls?

left: *Marzipan, released in 1999, was 3rd in the Classic Ballet Series, a very well-received line of dolls with collectors.*

right: *The beginning of the Mackie line—the 1990 release of Bob Mackie Gold. A primary audience for all things Barbie was shifting to adults.*

The Bob Mackie Era
(1990 - present)

Known primarily as the man who dresses Cher and other celebrities in vibrant, elaborate and daring fashions, Bob Mackie has excelled for more than a decade dressing his favorite petite model — Barbie — in dream designs. These glitzy dolls, which have always entranced the secondary market, literally drip with sequins, beads and rhinestones.

There's little dispute that the Mackie dolls epitomize glamour, transporting collectors to a fashion world they may never personally inhabit. Even the packaging continues the flavor of the dolls.

The Best Because?

The era of "Barbie doll as collectible" had begun in a big way. No longer was there concern that collectors wouldn't pay premium prices for a well-executed, limited-edition Barbie doll.

Not even the sky (or the Milan runways) were the limit. There was nothing too elegant, too pricey or too posh for Barbie dolls (or the collectors who love them).

left: *The Bob Mackie Platinum doll, released in 1991, naturally featured highly-detailed costuming.*
right: *Bob Mackie Starlight Splendor, also released in 1991, was the first black Barbie in the Mackie line.*

Bob Mackie Starlight Splendor

Model #2704
Hair Color: Black
Current Value: **$500 MIB**

Bob Mackie Neptune Fantasy

Model #4248
Hair Color: Blond
Current Value: **$750 MIB**

Detail is impeccable – nothing less than collectors would expect. Queen of Hearts sports a realistic beauty mark and striking lavender eyes; Starlight Splendor wears peacock-inspired eyeshadow; Neptune Fantasy literally swims in flowing sea-colored velvet.

Mackie's most recent Fantasy Goddess series depicted the allure and diversity of ethnic dress from Asia, Africa and other continents. Mackie has also created one-of-a-kind designs, like the 1997 Madame du Mischief, for Mattel's Dream Halloween auction.

left: *The 1992 Bob Mackie Neptune Fantasy is one of the most sought-after dolls in the series.*
right: *Fit for a fancy wedding… Bob Mackie Empress Bride was another 1992 release.*

Bob Mackie Empress Bride
Model #4247
Hair Color: Blond
Current Value: **$800 MIB**

left: *Bob Mackie Masquerade Ball,*
topped off with a huge feathered hat, was
the 1993 release.
opposite: *Costumed in a flowing red*
gown, the Bob Mackie Queen of Hearts
Barbie strode onto the scene in 1994.

Bob Mackie Masquerade Ball

Model #10803
Hair Color: Blond
Current Value: **$375 MIB**

Bob Mackie Queen of Hearts

Model #12046
Hair Color: Brunette
Current Value: **$275 MIB**

below: *The Bob Mackie Goddess of the Sun doll was the first in the "Goddess" group of the series.*

opposite: *Carrying her own crescent with her, the Bob Mackie Goddess of the Moon doll landed in collectors' hands in 1996.*

Bob Mackie
Goddess of the Sun
Model #14056
Hair Color: Blond
Current Value: **$200 MIB**

Bob Mackie
Goddess of the Moon
Model #14105
Current Value: **$180 MIB**

Bob Mackie Madame du Barbie

Model #17934
Hair Color: Blond
Current Value: **$250 MIB**

above: *This Marie Antoinette lookalike, Madame du Barbie, was a 1997 Bob Mackie release.*
opposite: *Another flamboyant doll (would we expect any less?) the 1998 Bob Mackie release Goddess of Asia.*

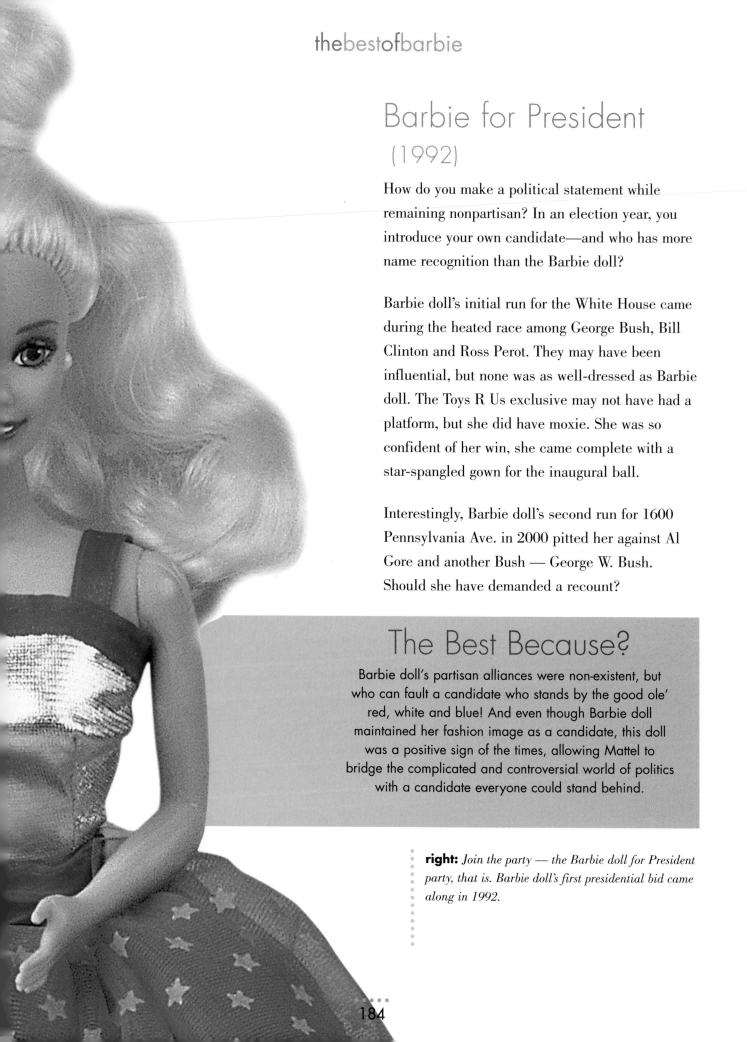

Barbie for President
(1992)

How do you make a political statement while remaining nonpartisan? In an election year, you introduce your own candidate—and who has more name recognition than the Barbie doll?

Barbie doll's initial run for the White House came during the heated race among George Bush, Bill Clinton and Ross Perot. They may have been influential, but none was as well-dressed as Barbie doll. The Toys R Us exclusive may not have had a platform, but she did have moxie. She was so confident of her win, she came complete with a star-spangled gown for the inaugural ball.

Interestingly, Barbie doll's second run for 1600 Pennsylvania Ave. in 2000 pitted her against Al Gore and another Bush — George W. Bush. Should she have demanded a recount?

The Best Because?

Barbie doll's partisan alliances were non-existent, but who can fault a candidate who stands by the good ole' red, white and blue! And even though Barbie doll maintained her fashion image as a candidate, this doll was a positive sign of the times, allowing Mattel to bridge the complicated and controversial world of politics with a candidate everyone could stand behind.

right: *Join the party — the Barbie doll for President party, that is. Barbie doll's first presidential bid came along in 1992.*

Barbie for President

Black doll, Model #3940
White doll, Model #3722
Hair Color: Blond
Current Value: **$65 MIB**

Fashion Luncheon Repro
Model #17382
Hair Color: Brown
Current Value: **$55 MIB**

Nostalgic Reproductions (1994-present)

Ain't nothin' like the real thing . . .

That mantra certainly holds true for collectors aching to get their hands on a Ponytail Barbie #1 or a rare, no longer produced fashion. But with rising prices, scarce supply and steady demand, owning a Barbie doll rarity isn't always realistic.

What, then, can Mattel do to quench collectors' demand for the look and quality of the past?

Beginning in 1994, Mattel issued its first reproduction of a vintage doll as part of its Nostalgic Series collection. Honoring the 35th anniversary of Barbie doll, this was a reproduction of the 1959 Ponytail #1. While not an exact replica (body markings are different and the packaging is clearly marked as a reproduction), the doll was just close enough to satisfy collectors who cherished the look of the Ponytails (but not their price tag).

Later reproductions featured vintage dolls in popular retro fashions like Silken Flame, Solo in the Spotlight, Busy Gal and Enchanted Evening.

In later years, the line was dubbed the Collector's Request series, culling their selections from—who better?—avid collectors.

The Best Because?

How dare they tamper with the best? While in other toy realms, reproductions are often frowned upon by collectors (correctly thinking, in some cases, that the prices of the originals would plummet), newer Barbie doll collectors often welcome finely-executed repros (even though collectors of true vintage Barbie dolls might shun them).

Prices for vintage Barbie doll rarities remain solid, even with repros in the field. The buyers are different, although no less passionate.

1962 FASHION AND DOLL REPRODUCTIONS

Collector Edition

left: *Almost as nice, for a fraction of the price. An easier on the budget way for Barbie collectors to accumulate their favorite dolls, reproductions entered the scene in 1994.*

right: *Reproduction doll Silken Flame.*

following spread: *Just a sampling of the repro Barbie dolls. The repro Ponytail #1 even has holes in her feet, like the original. Collectors can tell the difference with each model, although Busy Gal is very close to the original.*

Solo in the Spotlight
Model #13534/#13820
Hair Color: Blond/Brunette
Current Value: **$25 MIB**

30th Anniversary
Francie
Model #14808
Hair Color: Brunette
Current Value: **$45 MIB**

35th Anniversary
Barbie
Model #11590/#11782
Hair Color: Blond/Brunette
Current Value: **$50 MIB** (blond)
$80 MIB (brunette)

Poodle Parade
Model #15280
Hair Color: Brown
Current Value: **$55 MIB**

Sophisticated Lady
Model #24930
Hair Color: Blond
Current Value: **$60 MIB**

Busy Gal
Model #13675
Hair Color: Brunette
Current Value: **$55 MIB**

Pink Splendor
(1995)

The announcement of Pink Splendor's price tag echoed loudly in the ears of collectors who wondered if they had heard the news correctly.

Would Mattel really try to sell a Barbie doll for $900? After all, Barbie is a classic, but would collectors really bite at such a stratospheric retail price?

While few questioned the doll's lovely visage, enhanced by a Swarovski crystal-encrusted gown, few were willing (or able) to shell out the bucks for this stunner (plus, she took up a lot of space). A slow-to-buy circuit of dealers led to the doll being discounted immediately. Current secondary market value is around $400 to $500.

The Best Because?

This doll really tested of the mettle of collectors and may have subconsciously helped Mattel establish pricing boundaries. While retail prices of $100 to $200 are not uncommon for the higher-end dolls, it's unlikely a $900 retail price will be seen for a while, if ever.

left: *Even though Pink Splendor was remarkably well-detailed, she became discounted quickly.*
right: *This was definitely the test—the original retail price for Pink Splendor was $900.*

Pink Splendor
Model #16091
Hair Color: Blond
Current Value: **$550 MIB**

Share a Smile Becky in Wheelchair
(Toys R Us exlusive)

Model #15761
Hair Color: Reddish brown
Current Value: **$28 MIB**

Share a Smile Becky in Wheelchair (1997)

Mattel had deconstructed Barbie doll's intangible career barriers years before. But physical challenges had never been addressed until Mattel offered Barbie doll's friend Becky in a wheelchair as a Toys R Us exclusive.

barbie trivia

Political Bedfellows
The 2000 presidential election may have been in doubt for the real candidates, but the election marked the second time in history Barbie was on the ballot. A Barbie for President doll also appeared during the 1992 elections as a Toys R Us exclusive.

The Best Because?

Becky was a laudable addition to the Barbie doll universe. Now physically-challenged children would have a doll which more closely reflected their situations.

left: *Another advance from Mattel— Barbie doll's friend Becky as a physically-challenged doll complete with wheelchair.*

Billions of Dreams
(1997)

Just how many dreams has the Barbie doll inspired? Why, billions, of course! This striking limited-edition doll, with upswept hair and icy blue dress, was created to commemorate just that concept.

The Best Because?

Her look is timeless, her inspiration divine. She stands for everything Barbie dolls can be and little girls want to be.

left: *Details, details. Notice the Swarovski crystal earrings. A real gem for collectors.*
right: *Billions of Dreams was another commemorative release from Mattel in 1997.*

Billions of Dreams

Model #17641
Hair Color: Blond
Current Value: **$350 MIB**

Harley-Davidson Barbie #1

Model #17692
Hair Color: Blond
Current Value: **$400 MIB**

Harley-Davidson Line
(1997-present)

Take one longtime motorcycle success story. Add the beauty of Barbie dolls. Toss in a sassy dose of leather and denim . . . and hit the open road!

One thing this series also shows is the mainstream acceptance of Harley-Davidson. Popularized by Jay Leno and other recognizable celebs, the bikes became touted as American classics, almost as much as mom and apple pie. It's tough enough to imagine a line of Barbie dolls released in any earlier decade being associated with motorcycles and leather jackets *and* being Toys R Us exclusives, to boot.

Few licenses have such strong name recognition as Harley-Davidson, and even fewer hold the power to pair up with a powerhouse such as Barbie doll.

The marriage, however, has been strong enough to spawn seven dolls (five Barbie dolls and two Ken dolls) and an accessory such as a miniature Harley-Davidson Fat Boy motorcycle.

left: *First in a series, the Harley-Davidson Barbie was released in 1997 as a platinum blond.*
right: *The second Harley-Davidson Ken featured a full beard, shades, tattoo and chest hair.*
following spread: *Mattel's attention to detail is just part of the reason this series is a collector's favorite.*

Harley-Davidson Ken #2
Model #25638
Hair Color: Brown
Current Value: **$55 MIB**

The Best Because?

These dolls are a pure marketing coup de grace. Not all licensing agreements are as compatible or as enduring. Plus, Barbie doll just looks great in leather (and Ken doll's no scruff either).

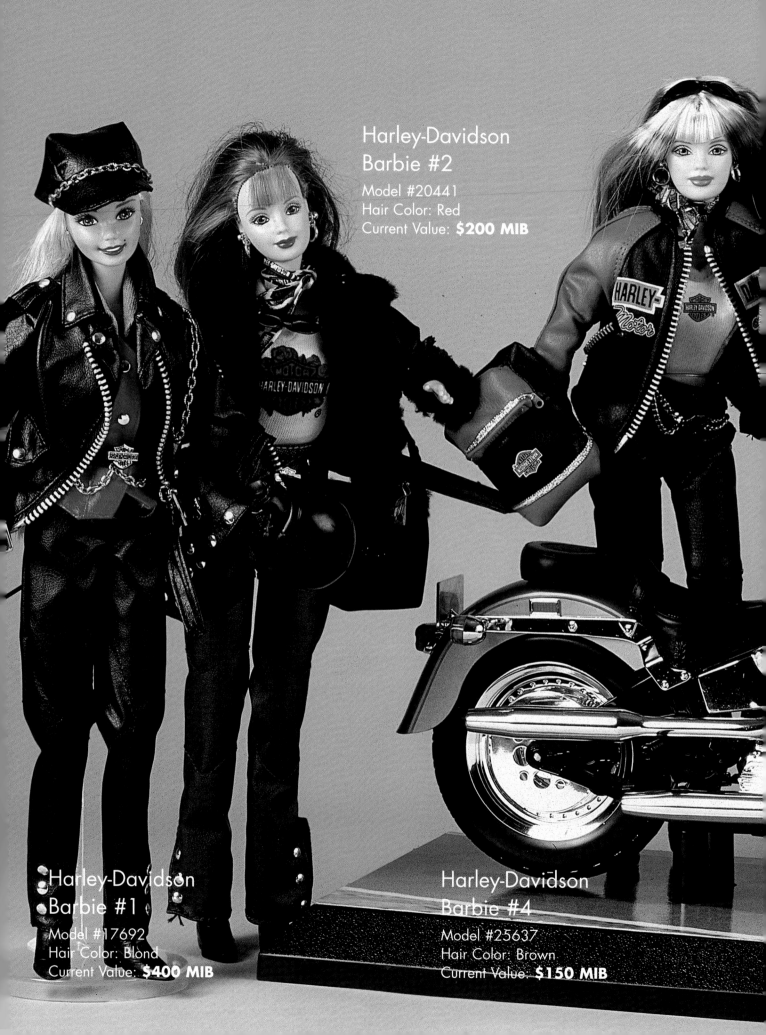

Harley-Davidson
Barbie #2
Model #20441
Hair Color: Red
Current Value: **$200 MIB**

Harley-Davidson
Barbie #1
Model #17692
Hair Color: Blond
Current Value: **$400 MIB**

Harley-Davidson
Barbie #4
Model #25637
Hair Color: Brown
Current Value: **$150 MIB**

Harley-Davidson
Ken #2
Model #25638
Hair Color: Brown
Current Value: **$55 MIB**

Harley-Davidson
Barbie #3
Model #22256
Hair Color: Black
Current Value: **$150 MIB**

Harley-Davidson
Ken #1
Model #22255
Hair Color: Brown
Current Value: **$100 MIB**

Winter in Montreal

Model #22258
Hair Color: Black
Current Value: **$50 MIB**

City Seasons

(1998-present)

You can take the girl out of the city…

In yet another attempt to freshen and modernize Barbie doll's fashion sense, the City Seasons series goes globetrotting to some of the most romanticized cities in the world like Tokyo, Rome, Paris and New York.

The Best Because?

Vicarious pleasure. Few collectors may have the means to actually spend spring in Tokyo or summer in Rome (or stylishly dress the part); these modestly-priced dolls cost less than a plane ticket or a Gucci suit, but might be just the fix.

left: *Winter in Montreal was one of the City Seasons' 1999 releases.*
right: *Just in time for the cherry blossoms, Spring in Tokyo, another City Seasons Barbie released in 1999.*

Spring in Tokyo

Model #19430
Hair Color: Brunette
Current Value: **$50 MIB**

Summer in Rome

Model #19431
Hair Color: Blond
Current Value: **$50 MIB**

top left: *Bella Barbie doll! The City Seasons Summer in Rome release, 1999.*
below: *Take in a show? Visit a world-famous gallery? Or just a fine dinner in midtown Manhattan? The 1998 Winter in New York City Seasons doll looks like she could do all three.*
far right: *This Barbie doll looks ready for a stroll along the Seine in this Autumn in Paris City Seasons 1998 release.*

Winter in New York

Model #19429
Hair Color: Blond
Current Value: **$50 MIB**

Autumn in Paris

Model #19367
Hair Color: Brunette
Current Value: **$50 MIB**

Great Fashions, Groovy Sixties
Model #27676
Hair Color: Red
Current Value: **$60 MIB**

Great Fashions of the 20th Century
(1998-present)

From the elegant, classy look one might wear on a Promenade in the Park in the early 1900s to the retro hipster attitude of the Peace and Love 1970s, Barbie doll's apparel has always reflected the times. Why not, then, create a series especially to spotlight these timeless looks?

Seven decades have been covered so far; and it will be interesting to see where the series goes from here.

The Best Because?

These dolls are miniature time capsules to the decades of the twentieth century, sometimes tinged with a touch of "what were we thinking?" And, as usual, these Barbie doll outfits are totally accurate.

left: *The Groovy Sixties Barbie, one of the Great Fashions of the 20th Century dolls. You can almost hear the go-go music in the background.*
right: *Mattel did an excellent job capturing the spirit of the times with the Great Fashions series.*

Kathleen Mary

Specially Made for

An Awesome Best Friend

by the makers of Barbie® doll

My Design™

friend of *Barbie*® doll

PERSONALITY PROFILE

Kathleen Mary has sparkling blue eyes and
wavy red hair. She is wearing her new
Radiant in Red Outfit with extra City Shopper
accessories. Her birthday is in June. She lives
in my neighborhood and spends a lot of time
playing. She's interested in movies, loves to
sing and enjoys being with all her friends.
Kathleen Mary is a special friend of Barbie,
personalized for you, An Awesome Best
Friend, from Lisa Jane!

Look for your
accessories inside
the package.

Your special
verification
number is

005 2885

My Design Dolls
(1999)

Did you ever want to be a friend of Barbie doll, but weren't sure how to make it happen?

Mattel's millennium-welcoming program, My Design, changed all that, for kids and adults alike.

Projecting one's interests, dreams and personality into a doll was one of principles Ruth Handler followed in creating the Barbie doll. The My Design program, until it was discontinued in 2000, allowed online buyers at *www.barbie.com* to customize (within strict boundaries) a doll bearing physical traits plugged into the program, thus becoming a friend of Barbie.

Name, backstory and personality traits are recorded on the doll's box. For $40, buyers could customize and order a doll in their likeness (or one for their niece Abby or Grandma Rose) and enter the world of being one of Barbie doll's friends.

barbie trivia

Zoo Too!
Barbie doll's entourage of pets has included dogs and cats, but her earliest pet was Dancer, a horse, in 1971.

left: *In 1999, dolls could be customized via the Barbie doll web site. Customizable dolls are a great gift idea, but their very individuality limits their collector value, at least for now.*

The Best Because?

What's not to love? An 11-1/2" doll of yourself, sans blemishes and bad language, dressed in garb your sister would kill for. It was an innovative program that connected Mattel to the online community.

It's unlikely My Design dolls will increase in value on the secondary market (after all, could anyone but you or your spouse want your eponymous doll?), but they remain a memorable addition to the world of dolls.

below: *First in the Together Forever Collection, the Romeo and Juliet gift set was released in 1998.*
right: *The Star Trek Barbie and Ken Gift Set, released in 1996.*

Barbie and Ken Gift Sets

What's the saying? Behind every good man is an even better woman? Whatever the spin, Mattel is perceptive enough to realize that Barbie and Ken dolls are a dynamic match in both formal occasions and casual events. They've capitalized on that sweet affinity for more than 30 years with gift sets featuring Barbie and Ken dolls in a variety of costumes.

Together Forever, Barbie and Ken as Romeo and Juliet
Model #19364
Current Value: **$100 MIB**

Star Trek Barbie and Ken
Model #15006
Current Value: **$30 MIB**

Together Forever, Barbie and Ken as King Arthur
and Queen Guinevere

Model #23880
Current Value: **$100 MIB**

The earliest sets, from the mid-1960s, paired the duo as parade leaders (the 1964 On Parade gift set) and bride and groom (Wedding Party). But it wasn't until the 1990s that gift sets featuring the sweethearts were aimed directly at collectors. These sets became increasingly more creative as Barbie and Ken morphed into TV stars (Star Trek, 1996; X-Files, 1998; Morticia and Gomez Addams, 2000; The Munsters, 2001), literary lovers (Romeo and Juliet, 1998; Phantom of the Opera, 1998) and mystical, magical pairs (King Arthur and Queen Guinevere, 1999; Merlin and Morgan LeFay, 2000; Sultan and Scherhazade, 2001).

The Best Because?

Even though they may don exotic garb and travel through time in these sets, underneath the costuming, they remain Barbie and Ken dolls. And it is that simple tenet that has kept the dolls' spirits and popularity intact for so many years.

Phantom of the Opera Gift Set, FAO Schwarz exclusive

Model #20377
Current Value: **$145 MIB**

left: *Mattel released the King Arthur and Guinevere Together Forever gift set in 1999. Interestingly, regular-issue dolls in the 1960s had costumes available by the same names, albeit not as detailed.*

right: *The Phantom of the Opera gift set was an FAO Schwarz exclusive. The popularity of the traveling show may account, in part, for Mattel releasing this set in 1998.*

Fashion Model
Delphine Barbie
Model #26929
Hair Color: Blond
Current Value: **$80 MIB**

word of the decade: **sophisticated**

What will Mattel unveil next for Barbie doll? She's already taken some big steps at the turn of the century. One of the most impressive Barbie dolls of all time, Lingerie Barbie from the Fashion Model series, brings Barbie full circle—back to her roots as a fashion model with a sophisticated look. The Hollywood Movie Star collection unveiled yet another persona for Barbie in the new millennium, and Wonder Woman took Barbie soaring to yet unscaled heights.

left: *The new century started with a new series—the Fashion Models. The value for Delphine Barbie is $80 MIB.*

right: *"Sophisticated" is the word of the decade when you see the Fashion Model series.*

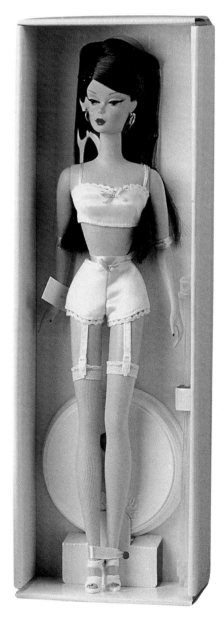

Barbie as Wonder Woman
(2000)

With all her guises, Barbie doll has lived as a hero many times over in her lifetime. But as the century turned, Mattel decided to make it official with the DC Comics-licensed Barbie as Wonder Woman, complete with golden lasso, jet black hair and star-studded cape. Paired with box art as bold as her persona, this doll crossed collectible genres to attract Barbie doll fans, comics aficionados and those who hoped a little of her power would rub off on them.

The Best Because?

Barbie as Wonder Woman made yet another daring statement about the heights to which Barbie doll could go — heck, if she could fly, she truly could do anything.

left: *No need for this doll to use her golden lasso on collectors — they bought in droves — and that's the truth.*
right: *Probably one of Mattel's greatest forays into the world of pop culture, Barbie as Wonder Woman has been a huge hit.*

Barbie as™ Wonder Woman

Model #24638
Hair Color: Black
Current Value: **$50 MIB**

Fashion Model Series, Lingerie #1
Model #26930
Hair Color: Blond
Current Value: **$40 MIB**

Fashion Model Series
(2000)

The millennium may have come in on little cat feet, but Barbie doll was roaring like a tiger. And it was obvious Mattel had put a lot of time, research and design into its newest model for her walk down the 21st-century catwalk.

Daring new face paints and hair colors notwithstanding, the jewel of this modern line was the debut of "Silkstone," a revolutionary composition. The Fashion Model dolls are made of this magical material that looks and feels like porcelain but remains smooth and more durable.

Since 1959, "fashion" has remained Barbie doll's middle name. Retro in flavor (in both look and fashions), these dolls hark back to Barbie doll's roots while unveiling her as a supermodel for the millennium.

Three lingerie dolls highlight the line. Other dolls in the line recall the demeanor, style and eloquence of movie stars like Grace Kelly and Veronica Lake.

barbie trivia

Who was the first designer to have a signature on a Barbie fashion?
- Bob Mackie
- Oscar de la Renta
- Anne Klein
- Ralph Lauren

Answer: In 1985, Oscar de la Renta designed exciting and daring Barbie fashions. It wasn't until several years later that Bob Mackie began designing his coveted fashions for Barbie.

The Best Because?

A decidedly daring look. A ravishingly brash attitude. A revolutionary new material. They modernize Barbie doll while honoring her past and set a new standard of quality for collectible dolls.

left: *Note the look of the "Silkstone" material for the bodies of these new dolls. An excellent innovation.*

epilogue

. . . .

where are you going?

where have you been?

The title of this epilogue, which I respectfully borrow from my favorite Joyce Carol Oates' short story, is an appropriate phrase to close *The Best of Barbie*. Why?

The more I researched more than 40 years of Barbie dolls, looked at their faces, handled the dolls and visited the collections, the more I understood that Barbie doll's future is plainly motivated by (although not inhibited by) her past. She has, in many ways, come full circle. Back to her fashion roots. Back to, in some cases, a more vintage look. Back to being a vessel for imagination, dreams and wonderment.

So what, then, is the best way to gauge Barbie doll's future?

All you have to do is look at the face of an early Ponytail Barbie or a modern Lingerie doll. Their sophisticated appearance creates the mystery that *is* Barbie doll. Is she smiling? Is she secretly spying on a nearby paramour? What will she do next?

That, in a nutshell (or, in Barbie doll's case, in a hatbox), is the essence and enigma of Barbie as she greets the 21st century. She certainly knows where she's been, and chances are she has a pretty good idea where she's going.

And while Barbie doll designers probably have the next three to five years of fashions and faces mapped out, they, like the dolls, remain stoic, untelling . . .

. . . but don't worry — when the time is right, Barbie doll will always have plenty to say.

left: *Fashion Model Lingerie #2.*

bestwords

glossary of terms

American Girl:

The name used to refer to the style of doll introduced in 1965. She featured a chin-length bobbed hairstyle.

Baggie Dolls:

This refers to dolls from the 1970s that were repacked in plastic bags instead of boxes. Most were previously-issued or overstocked dolls.

Bubblecut:

The short, styled bob hairstyle found on most dolls made from 1961-1967. Some of these dolls featured hair parted on the side. These are called "sideparts."

left: *Student Teacher Barbie, from 1965, seems like the perfect doll to introduce the terms every student of Barbie should know.*
right: *American Girl is a collector's favorite.*

Color Magic:

Introduced in 1966, this doll featured brilliant hair colors that could be changed with a special solution supplied by Mattel.

Designer Dolls:

The term used to refer to dolls wearing costumes by top fashion designers like Bob Mackie, Anne Klein and Oscar de la Renta.

Dressed Box Dolls:

Most Barbie dolls were sold dressed in swimsuits. The term "dressed box" refers to 1960s dolls in a striped box already dressed in an official Mattel outfit. Not all outfits were offered on dolls in this fashion.

Exclusive:

The term given to a doll that is limited in distribution to a particular store or outlet, such as Toys R Us or FAO Schwarz.

Flocked Hair:

The fuzzy hair found on the first Ken doll.

Greasy Face Syndrome:

Because of the vinyl used on some Ponytail dolls, these vintage dolls often have greasy faces, denoting a breakdown in the vinyl over time.

Green Ear Syndrome:

Metal earrings left in vintage Barbie dolls eventually corroded and turned the vinyl ears green.

High color:

A phrase used to describe dolls, like the Color Magics, with especially bright lip and cheek color.

MIB:

An abbreviation for Mint in Box.

MIP:

An abbreviation for Mint in Package.

NRFB:

An abbreviation for Never Removed from Box.

Pilgrim:

A style of Barbie pump shoe

Pink Box Dolls:

This term refers to the more commonly-found, inexpensive regular issue Barbie dolls made by Mattel, as opposed to their higher-end collector editions.

above left: *Goddess of the Moon, one of the Bob Mackie designer dolls.*

Pink Silhouette Box:

This pink box, with white and gray Barbie doll silhouettes, featured early Ponytail dolls dressed in outfits for store display only. The dolls were not normally sold in these boxes.

Repro:

The shortened form of the word "reproduction," it refers to the reissues of early Barbie dolls or fashions made for the collectors' market.

Ponytail:

The hairstyle found on the earliest Barbie dolls. That name, however, was never used by Mattel. It is the term collectors have come to universally accept for the early dolls with ponytailed hair.

Sidepart:

A hairstyle parted on the side.

Silkstone:

Type of vinyl introduced in Mattel's Fashion Doll series of 2000. The smooth vinyl has the silky feel and heft of porcelain but remains more durable.

Titian:

Often used to describe the light-red hair found on some Barbie dolls.

Twist 'n Turn:

This body style, featuring a swivel waist, was introduced in 1967. The dolls also featured a new head mold, makeup and hairstyle.

left: *Fashion Luncheon reproduction.*
right: *Twist 'n Turn Barbie.*

The OFFICIAL Barbie Doll Collect

December 2000

Barbie
Bazaar

Collector's Magazine $4.95

Countdown to
40 Years With
KEN

Vintage
**BLACK
DOLLS**

BMAA
Voting

Collectible
New Dolls

...port
**BMAA
Voting**

*Beauty's
Triumph*

bestbets

additional resources

Barbie doll collectors are never alone. They give a positive and impressive meaning to the word "network" since they find so many ways to communicate with each other. Books, magazines, Web sites and clubs are plentiful. While not a complete list, here is a look at some of the "best bets" for Barbie doll collectors today.

Publications

Several publications cater to doll lovers; one is specifically devoted to Barbie doll fans. Check out these fine print resources.

Barbie Bazaar
Murat-Caviale, Inc.
5617 Sixth Avenue
Kenosha, WI 53140
(262) 658-1004
www.barbiebazaar.com

Doll Reader
6405 Flank Dr.
Harrisburg, PA 17112-2753
www.dollreader.com

Dolls Magazine
P.O. Box 1972
Marion, OH 43305

Toy Shop
700 E. State St.
Iola, WI 54990
(715) 445-2214
www.toyshopmag.com

Auction Houses

Collectors often turn to auction houses to buy and sell Barbie dolls, accessories and collections. Two of the major doll auction venues are

McMasters Doll Auctions
P.O. Box 1755
Cambridge, OH 43725
(800) 842-3526
www.mcmastersauctions.com

Theriault's, The Doll Masters
P.O. Box 151
Annapolis, MD 21401
(800) 638-0422
www.theriaults.com

Clubs

Literally hundreds of clubs, ranging from local and regional to national and international, exist to serve avid collectors. The Barbie doll resources listed on this page are the best bets for locating other collectors and clubs.

Web Sites

This list could be endless, especially with all the dealer, retail, secondary market and fan sites out there. The best bet for surfing through the sites more successfully is to search the Internet under the keywords "Barbie," "Barbie dolls," "Barbie collectibles," "Mattel's Barbie" or other appropriate terms.

Mattel, Inc.
www.barbie.com
www.barbiecollectibles.com

About.com
Collectdolls.about.com
This site will provide collectors with many links to clubs, Web sites and other Barbie resources.

Books

Books on America's favorite fashion doll icon are plentiful as well. A library search or visit to *www.bn.com* or *www.amazon.com* will also reveal more complete lists of Barbie books. Here are some favorites.

The Ultimate Barbie Doll Book
Marcie Melillo (Krause Publications, 1996)

The Collectible Barbie Doll, Second Edition
Janine Fennick (Running Press/Courage, 1999)

Fashion Doll Price Guide 2000-2001
(Portfolio Press, 2000)

Collector's Compass Barbie Doll
(Martingale & Company, 2000)

Barbie: A Visual Guide to the Ultimate Fashion Doll
(DK Publishing, 2000)

The Story of Barbie Doll, Second Edition
Kitturah B. Westenhouser (Collector Books, 1999)

The Collectors Encyclopedia of Barbie Dolls and Collectibles
Sibyl DeWein and Joan Ashabraner
(Collector Books, 1994 ed.)

Contemporary Barbie
Jane Sarasohn-Kahn (Antique Trader Books, 1997)

Identifying Barbie Dolls: The New Compact Study
Guide and Identifier
Janine Fennick (1998)

The Barbie Doll Years: A Comprehensive Listing
and Value Guide of Dolls and Accessories
Patrick C. Olds and Joyce L. Olds
(Collector Books, 2000)

Face of the American Dream:
Barbie Doll 1959-1971
Christopher Varaste (Hobby House, 1999)

Butterfly Art Barbie, 1999, $15 MIB

priceguide

Prices listed are for dolls in Mint No Box (MNB) and Mint in Box Box (MIB) condition. Page numbers are included for dolls pictured in *The Best of Barbie*.

The "Barbie & Friends" section includes vintage and modern regular-issue and pink box dolls. Collector and limited-edition dolls (vintage and modern store exclusives and gift sets) and porcelain dolls follow under their respective headings under "Collector Editions & Store Exclusives."

Barbie & Friends dolls

	MNB	MIB	Page #
All American Barbie, 1991, No. 9423	4	20	
All American Christie, 1991, No. 9425	4	25	
All American Ken, 1991, No. 9424	4	15	
All American Kira, 1991, No. 9427	4	20	
All American Teresa, 1991, No. 9426	4	30	
All Star Ken, 1981, No. 3553	7	25	
All Stars Barbie, 1989, No. 9099	5	25	
All Stars Christie, 1989, No. 9352	5	20	
All Stars Ken, 1989, No. 9361	5	20	
All Stars Midge, 1989, No. 9360	5	30	
All Stars Teresa, 1989, No. 9353	5	30	
Allan, bendable leg, 1965, No. 1010	150	400	
Allan, straight leg, 1964, No. 1000	55	125	
American Beauties Mardi Gras Barbie, 1988, No. 4930	40	100	
American Beauties Army Barbie, 1989, No. 3966	20	40	130
American Beauty Queen, 1991, No. 3137	5	45	
American Beauty Queen, black, 1991, No. 3245	5	35	
American Girl (see Bendable Leg)			
Angel Face Barbie, 1982, No. 5640	8	40	
Animal Lovin' Barbie, black, 1989, No. 4828	5	75	
Animal Lovin'Barbie, white, 1989, No. 1350	5	40	
Animal Lovin'Ken, 1989, No. 1351	5	20	
Animal Lovin'Nikki, 1989, No. 1352	7	20	
Astronaut Barbie, black, 1985, No. 1207	30	40	
Astronaut Barbie, white, 1985, No. 2449	25	75	
Babysitter Courtney, 1991, No. 9434	4	15	
Babysitter Skipper, 1991, No. 9433	4	15	
Babysitter Skipper, black, 1991, No. 1599	4	10	
Baggie Casey, blond (sold in plastic bag), 1975, No. 9000	75	250	
Ballerina Barbie on Tour, gold, 1st version, 1976, No. 9613	45	125	
Ballerina Barbie, 1st version, 1976, No. 9093	20	65	
Ballerina Cara, 1976, No. 9528	25	65	
Barbie & Her Fashion Fireworks, 1976, No. 9805	20	60	
Barbie & the Beat, 1990, No. 3751	5	30	
Barbie & the Beat Christie, 1990, No. 2752	5	15	
Barbie & the Beat Midge, 1990, No. 2754	6	20	

Barbie & Friends dolls

	MNB	MIB	Page #
Barbie Hair Happenings (department store exclusive, red head), 1971, No. 1174	400	1,000	
Barbie with Growin' Pretty Hair, 1971, No. 1144	100	300	96-97
Bathtime Fun Barbie, 1991, No. 9601	3	20	
Bathtime Fun Barbie, black, 1991, No. 9603	3	15	
Beach Blast Barbie, 1989, No. 3237	3	20	
Beach Blast Christie, 1989, No. 3253	4	15	
Beach Blast Ken, 1989, No. 3238	4	15	
Beach Blast Miko, 1989, No. 3244	4	15	
Beach Blast Skipper, 1989, No. 3242	4	15	
Beach Blast Steven, 1989, No. 3251	4	15	
Beach Blast Teresa, 1989, No. 3249	5	15	
Beautiful Bride Barbie, 1978, No. 9907	60	125	
Beauty Secrets Barbie, 1st issue, 1980, No. 1290	12	65	
Beauty Secrets Christie, 1980, No. 1295	12	65	
Beauty, Barbie's Dog, 1979, No. 1018	12	30	

Bendable Leg "American Girl"

	MNB	MIB	Page #
Bendable Leg "American Girl" Barbie, short hair, 1965, No. 1070	850	1,900	44-45, 82, 85
Bendable Leg "American Girl" Barbie, Color Magic Face, 1966, No. 1070	1,300	2,900	
Bendable Leg "American Girl" Barbie, long hair, 1965, No. 1070	1,300	2,800	
Bendable Leg "American Girl" Barbie, side-part long hair, 1966, No. 1070	2,400	4,000	
Bendable Leg "American Girl" Barbie, Swirl Ponytail or Bubblecut hairstyle, 1965, No. 1070	950	3,000	
Benetton Barbie, 1991, No. 9404	6	45	
Benetton Christie, 1991, No. 9407	6	35	
Benetton Marina, 1991, No. 9409	6	35	
Black Barbie, 1980, No. 1293	30	100	138-139
Brad, bendable leg, 1970, No. 1142	75	150	
Brad, talking, 1970, No. 1114	65	150	

Bubblecut Barbie dolls

	MNB	MIB	Page #
Bubblecut Barbie Sidepart, all hair colors, 1961, No. 850	425	900	80

Barbie & Friends dolls | MNB | MIB | Page

Bubblecut Barbie, blond, brunette,
titian, 1962, No. 850 . . . . .150 . . . . .350 — *30*
Bubblecut Barbie,
brunette, 1961, No. 850 . . . . . . .900 . . . .1,400 — *31, 80*
Bubblecut Barbie,
white ginger, 1962, No. 850 . . . . .450 900
Busy Barbie, 1971, No. 3311 . . . . . . .100 . . . .300 — *102-103*
Busy Francie, 1971, No. 3313 . . . . . . .175 . . . .425 — *107*
Busy Ken, 1971, No. 3314 . . . . .60 . . . .165 — *104*
Busy Steffie, 1971, No. 3312 . . . . . . .125 . . . .350 — *106*
Butterfly Art Barbie, 1999 . . . . .5 . . . .15 — *236*
Calgary Olympic Skating Barbie,
1987, No. 4547 . . . . .25 60
California Dream Barbie,
1988, No. 4439 . . . . .5 20
California Dream Christie,
1988, No. 4443 . . . . .6 15
California Dream Ken,
1988, No. 4441 . . . . .8 15
California Dream Midge,
1988, No. 4442 . . . . .3 15
California Dream Skipper,
1988, No. 4440 . . . . .13 20
California Dream Teresa,
1988, No. 4403 . . . . .15 20
Carla, European exclusive,
1976, No. 7377 . . . . .65 140
Casey, Twist and Turn,
1967, No. 1180 . . . . .85 275
Chris, titian, blond, brunette
(Tutti's friend), 1967, No. 3570 . . .65 250
Christie, talking, 1970, No. 1126 . . . .65 . . . .200 — *53*
Christie, Twist N Turn, 1970, No. 1119 125 500
Coach Ken & Tommy,
white or black, 2000 . . . . .7 15

Midge doll, straight leg, 1963, $175 MIB

Barbie & Friends dolls | MNB | MIB | Page

Color Magic Barbie, Golden Blond,
1966, No. 1150 . . . . .650 . . . .2,400 — *46-47*
Color Magic Barbie, Midnight Black,
1966, No. 1150 . . . . .1,200 . . . .3,500 — *46*
Cool City Blues: Barbie, Ken, Skipper,
1989, No. 4893 . . . . .20 45
Cool Shavin'Ken, 1996, No. 15469 . . . .10 15
Cool Times Barbie, 1989, No. 3022 . . . .5 25
Cool Times Christie, 1989, No. 3217 . . . .5 20
Cool Times Ken, 1989, No. 3219 . . . . . .5 20
Cool Times Midge, 1989, No. 3216 . . . .7 20
Cool Times Teresa, 1989, No. 3218 . . . .9 20
Cool Tops Courtney, 1989, No. 7079 . . . .7 20
Cool Tops Kevin, 1989, No. 9351 . . . . . .5 20
Cool Tops Skipper, black,
1989, No. 5441 . . . . .5 15
Cool Tops Skipper, white,
1989, No. 4989 . . . . .7 15
Corduroy Cool Barbie,
2000, No. 24658 . . . . .5 10
Costume Ball Barbie, black,
1991, No. 7134 . . . . .6 15
Costume Ball Barbie, white,
1991, No. 7123 . . . . .6 25
Costume Ball Ken, black,
1991, No. 7160 . . . . .6 20
Costume Ball Ken, white,
1991, No. 7154 . . . . .6 30
Crystal Barbie, black, 1984, No. 4859 . .10 25
Crystal Barbie, white, 1984, No. 4598 . .10 35
Crystal Ken, black, 1983, No. 9036 . . . .15 25
Crystal Ken, white, 1983, No. 4898 . . . .8 30
Dance Club Barbie, 1989, No. 3509 . . . .5 45
Dance Club Devon, 1989, No. 3513 . . . .5 40
Dance Club Kayla, 1989, No. 3512 . . . .5 85
Dance Club Ken, 1989, No. 3511 . . . . . .5 40
Dance Magic Barbie, 1990, No. 4836 . . .7 25
Dance Magic Barbie, black,
1990, No. 7080 . . . . .7 25
Dance Magic Ken, 1990, No. 7081 . . . . .6 20
Dance Magic Ken, black,
1990, No. 7082 . . . . .6 20
Day-to-Night Barbie, black,
1985, No. 7945 . . . . .10 35
Day-to-Night Barbie, Hispanic,
1985, No. 7944 . . . . .17 40
Day-to-Night Barbie, white,
1985, No. 7929 . . . . .10 40
Day-to-Night Ken, black,
1984, No. 9018 . . . . .8 20
Day-to-Night Ken, white,
1984, No. 9019 . . . . .8 25
Dentist Barbie, 1997, No. 17255 . . . . . .15 30
Doctor Barbie, 1988, No. 3850 . . . . . . .8 45
Doctor Ken, 1988, No. 4118 . . . . .5 40

Dolls of the World/International

Arctic, 1997, No. 16495 . . . . .20 30
Australian, two box variations,
1993, No. 3626 . . . . .10 35
Austrian, 1999, No. 21553 . . . . .15 25
Brazillian, 1990, No. 9094 . . . . .15 60
Canadian, 1988, No. 4928 . . . . .15 75
Chilean, 1998, No. 18559 . . . . .10 20
Chinese, 1994, No. 11180 . . . . .10 30
Czechoslovakian, 1991, No. 7330 . . . . .30 110
Dutch, 1994, No. 11104 . . . . .10 35

Barbie & Friends dolls

	MNB	MIB	Page #
English, 1992, No. 4973	12	80	
Eskimo, 1982, No. 3898	30	100	
Eskimo, 1991, No. 9844	8	60	
French, 1997, No. 16499	10	25	
German, 1987, No. 3188	45	100	
German, 1995, No. 12598	10	25	
Ghanaian, 1996, No. 15303	15	25	
Gift Set (Chinese, Dutch, Kenyan), 1994, No. 12043	30	70	
Gift Set (Irish, German, Polynesian), 1995, No. 13939	30	65	
Gift Set (Japanese, Indian, Norwegian), 1996, No. 15283	30	60	
Greek, 1986, No. 2997	30	80	
Iceland, 1987, No. 3189	30	100	
Indian, 1982, No. 3897	50	120	
Indian, 1995, No. 14451	12	25	
Irish, 1984, No. 7517	45	115	*152-153, 157*
Irish, 1995, No. 12998	10	40	
Italian, 1980, No. 1602	65	175	*154, 156*
Italian, 1993, No. 2256	10	50	
Jamaican, silver earrings, 1992, No. 4647	12	55	
Japanese, 1985, No. 9481	55	125	*136-137, 157*
Japanese, 1996, No. 14163	10	20	
Kenyan, 1994, No. 11181	10	35	*157*
Korean, 1988, No. 4929	15	75	
Malaysian, 1991, No. 7329	10	50	
Mexican, 1989, No. 1917	15	50	
Mexican, 1995, No. 14449	10	20	
Moroccan, 1999, No. 21507	15	25	
Native American #1, two box versions, 1993, No. 1753	12	45	
Native American #2, 1994, No. 11609	10	35	
Native American #3, 1995, No. 12699	10	30	
Nigerian, 1990, No. 7376	15	60	*156*
Norwegian, pink flowers, limited to 3,000, 1996, No. 14450	12	65	
NW Coast Native American Barbie, 2000, No. 24671	12	25	
Oriental, 1981, No. 3262	55	130	
Parisian, 1980, No. 1600	65	150	*157*
Parisian, 1991, No. 9843	8	60	
Peruvian, 1986, No. 2995	30	80	
Peruvian, 1999, No. 21506	15	25	
Polish, 1998, No. 18560	15	25	
Polynesian, 1995, No. 12700	10	30	
Princess of India, 2000, No. 28374	8	20	
Princess of the French Court, 2000, No. 28372	8	20	
Princess of the Incas, 2000, No. 28373	8	20	
Puerto Rican, 1997, No. 16754	15	25	
Royal, 1980, No. 1601	65	175	*155, 156*
Russian, 1989, No. 1916	20	25	
Russian, 1997, No. 16500	20	75	
Scottish, 1981, No. 3263	50	130	
Scottish, 1991, No. 9845	8	60	
Spanish, 1983, No. 4031	40	110	
Spanish, 1992, No. 4963	12	45	
Spanish, 2000, No. 24670	12	25	
Swedish, 1983, No. 4032	35	100	
Swedish, 2000, No. 24672	12	25	
Swiss, 1984, No. 7451	35	100	
Thai, 1998, No. 18561	10	20	

Barbie & Friends dolls

	MNB	MIB	Page #
Dramatic New Living Barbie, 1970, No. 1116	75	275	*94-95*
Dramatic New Living Skipper, 1970, No. 1117	50	175	
Dream Bride, 1992, No. 1623	10	40	
Dream Date Barbie, 1983, No. 5868	10	25	*16, 142-143*
Dream Date Ken, 1983, No. 4077	10	25	
Dream Glow Barbie, black, 1986, No. 2242	12	25	
Dream Glow Barbie, Hispanic, 1986, No. 1647	25	70	
Dream Glow Barbie, white, 1986, No. 2248	12	45	
Dream Glow Ken, black, 1986, No. 2421	13	20	
Dream Glow Ken, white, 1986, No. 2250	13	15	
Dream Time Barbie, pink, 1985, No. 9180	10	25	
Earring Magic Barbie, blond, 1993, No. 7014	15	25	
Earring Magic Ken, 1993, No. 2290	15	40	*163, 166-167*
Fabulous Fur Barbie, 1983, No. 7093	20	65	
Fashion Jeans Barbie, 1981, No. 5313	15	65	
Fashion Jeans Ken, 1982, No. 5316	12	25	
Fashion Photo Barbie, two versions, 1978, No. 2210	20	75	
Fashion Photo Christie, 1978, No. 2324	20	75	
Fashion Photo P.J., 1978, No. 2323	35	85	
Fashion Play Barbie, 1983, No. 7193	10	30	
Fashion Play Barbie, 1987, No. 4835	10	25	
Fashion Play Barbie, 1990, No. 9429	2	30	
Fashion Play Barbie, 1991, No. 9629	2	20	
Fashion Play Barbie, black, 1991, No. 5953	2	15	
Fashion Play Barbie, Hispanic, 1990, No. 5954	2	15	
Fashion Queen Barbie, 1963, No. 870	145	500	*38-39*
Feelin'Fun Barbie, two versions, white, 1st issue, 1988, No. 1189	5	20	
Flight Time Barbie, black, 1990, No. 9916	5	20	
Flight Time Barbie, white, 1990, No. 9584	5	30	
Flight Time Ken, 1990, No. 9600	5	20	
Fluff, 1971, No. 1143	100	210	
Francie with Growin'Pretty Hair, 1971, No. 1129	75	225	
Francie, bendable leg, blond, brunette, 1966, No. 1130	150	350	*68*
Francie, Hair Happenins, 1970, No. 1122	150	400	
Francie, straight leg, brunette, blond, 1966, No. 1140	150	400	*69*
Francie, Twist N Turn, "Black Francie" 1st issue, red hair, 1967, No. 1100	900	1,600	
Francie, Twist N Turn, "Black Francie" 2nd issue, black hair, No. 1100	900	1,500	*71*
Francie, Twist N Turn, blond or brunette, "No Bangs", 1967, No. 1170	650	1,200	*70*
Francie, Twist N Turn, blond or brunette, long hair with bangs, 1969, No. 1170	150	450	
Francie, Twist N Turn, blond or brunette, short hair, 1969, No. 1170	200	500	

Barbie & Friends dolls

	MNB	MIB	Page #
Free Moving Barbie, 1974, No. 7270	.50	.100	*116-117*
Free Moving Cara, 1974, No. 7283	.65	.125	
Free Moving Ken, 1974, No. 7280	.50	.75	*116*
Free Moving P.J., 1974, No. 7281	.50	.85	
Funtime Barbie, black, 1987, No. 1739	.5	.25	
Funtime Barbie, white, 1987, No. 1738	.5	.25	
Funtime Ken, 1987, No. 7194	.7	.20	
Garden Party Barbie, 1989, No. 1953	.8	.18	
Gift Giving Barbie, 1986, No. 1922	.5	.30	
Gift Giving Barbie, 1989, No. 1205	.5	.30	
Gold Medal Olympic Barbie Skater, 1975, No. 7262	.20	.100	
Gold Medal Olympic Barbie Skier, 1975, No. 7264	.20	.100	
Gold Medal Olympic P.J. Gymnast, 1975, No. 7263	.20	.85	
Gold Medal Olympic Skier Ken, 1975, No. 7261	.20	.85	
Gold Medal Olympic Skipper, 1975, No. 7274	.20	.85	
Golden Dreams Barbie, two versions, 1981, No. 1974	.15	.60	
Golden Dreams Christie, 1981, No. 3249	.15	.65	
Great Shapes Barbie, black, 1984, No. 7834	.5	.25	
Great Shapes Barbie, w/Walkman, 1984, No. 7025	.12	.40	
Great Shapes Barbie, white, 1984, No. 7025	.5	.35	
Great Shapes Ken, 1984, No. 7310	.5	.25	
Great Shapes Skipper, 1984, No. 7417	.5	.25	
Groom Todd, 1982, No. 4253	.15	.45	
Growin' Pretty Hair Barbie, 1971, No. 1144	.150	.350	
Growing Up Ginger, 1977, No. 9222	.30	.140	
Growing Up Skipper, 1977, No. 7259	.30	.150	*162, 168-169*
Happy Birthday Barbie, 1981, No. 1922	.8	.45	
Happy Birthday Barbie, 1984, No. 1922	.8	.35	
Happy Birthday Barbie, 1991, No. 9561	.8	.20	
Happy Birthday Barbie, black, 1991, No. 9561	.8	.30	
Hawaiian Barbie, 1975, No. 7470	.25	.68	
Hawaiian Barbie, 1977, No. 7470	.30	.80	
Hawaiian Fun Barbie, 1991, No. 5040	.3	.20	
Hawaiian Fun Christie, 1991, No. 5044	.3	.20	
Hawaiian Fun Jazzie, 1991, No. 9294	.3	.20	
Hawaiian Fun Ken, 1991, No. 5041	.3	.15	
Hawaiian Fun Kira, 1991, No. 5043	.3	.15	
Hawaiian Fun Skipper, 1991, No. 5042	.3	.15	
Hawaiian Fun Steven, 1991, No. 5045	.3	.15	
Hawaiian Ken, 1979, No. 2960	.13	.50	
Hawaiian Ken, 1984, No. 7495	.7	.30	
High School Chelsie, 1989, No. 3698	.5	.20	
High School Dude, Jazzie's boyfriend, 1989, No. 3600	.5	.20	
High School Jazzie, 1989, No. 3635	.5	.20	
High School Stacie, 1989, No. 3636	.5	.20	
Hispanic Barbie, 1980, No. 1292	.15	.75	*140-141*
Hollywood Nails Barbie, white or black, 1999	.7	.15	
Hollywood Nails Teresa, white or black, 1999	.7	.15	
Home Pretty Barbie, 1990, No. 2249	.8	.18	
Homecoming Queen Skipper, black, 1988, No. 2390	.8	.20	
Homecoming Queen Skipper, white, 1988, No. 1952	.12	.25	

Barbie & Friends dolls

	MNB	MIB	Page #
Horse Lovin' Barbie, 1983, No. 1757	.10	.40	
Horse Lovin' Ken, 1983, No. 3600	.8	.25	
Horse Lovin' Skipper, 1983, No. 5029	.8	.25	
Hot Stuff Skipper, 1984, No. 7927	.5	.18	
Ice Capades Barbie, 50th Anniversary, black, 1990, No. 7348	.5	.25	
Ice Capades Barbie, 50th Anniversary, white, 1990, No. 7365	.5	.35	
Ice Capades Ken, 1990, No. 7375	.5	.25	
Inline Skating Barbie, 1996, No. 15473	.5	.25	
Inline Skating Ken, 1996, No. 15474	.5	.25	
Inline Skating Midge, 1996, No. 15475	.5	.25	
Island Fun Barbie, 1988, No. 4061	.3	.20	
Island Fun Christie, 1988, No. 4092	.3	.20	
Island Fun Ken, 1988, No. 4060	.3	.15	
Island Fun Skipper, 1988, No. 4064	.3	.15	
Island Fun Steven, 1988, No. 4093	.3	.15	
Island Fun Teresa, 1988, No. 4117	.3	.15	
Jazzie Workout, 1989, No. 3633	.5	.12	
Jewel Girl Barbie, Christie, Teresa (new body style, belly button), 2000	.15	.30	
Jewel Secrets Barbie, black, two box versions, 1987, No. 1756	.6	.55	
Jewel Secrets Barbie, white, two box versions, 1987, No. 1737	.6	.35	
Jewel Secrets Ken, black, 1987, No. 3232	.6	.25	
Jewel Secrets Ken, rooted hair, 1987, No. 1719	.6	.25	
Jewel Secrets Skipper, 1987, No. 3133	.6	.25	
Jewel Secrets Whitney, 1987, No. 3179	.8	.25	
Julia, talking, first issue with straight hair, 1969, No. 1128	.85	.250	
Julia, talking, second issue, Afro hair, 1969, No. 1128	.85	.250	
Julia, Twist N Turn, one-piece nurse dress, 2nd issue, 1969, No. 1127	.100	.250	
Julia, Twist N Turn, two-piece nurse outfit, 1st issue, 1969, No. 1127	.125	.300	
Ken, bendable leg, brunette, 1965, No. 750	.155	.300	*37*
Ken, bendable leg, talking, 1970, No. 1124	.60	.125	
Ken, flocked hair, brunette, blond, 1961, No. 750	.100	.200	*32-33*
Ken, painted hair, brunette, blond, 1962, No. 750	.50	.175	*34*
Kevin, 1991, No. 9325	.5	.10	
Kissing Barbie, 1979, No. 2597	.8	.65	*118*
Kissing Christie, 1979, No. 2955	.10	.65	
Lights & Lace Barbie, 1991, No. 9725	.4	.30	
Lights & Lace Christie, 1991, No. 9728	.4	.30	
Lights & Lace Teresa, 1991, No. 9727	.4	.25	
Live Action Barbie, 1970, No. 1155	.60	.150	*89, 90-91,93*
Live Action Barbie Onstage, 1970, No. 1152	.75	.250	
Live Action Christie, 1970, No. 1175	.60	.250	*92*
Live Action Ken, 1970, No. 1159	.55	.150	*93*
Live Action Ken on Stage, 1970, No. 1172	.40	.150	
Live Action P.J., 1970, No. 1156	.65	.250	*92*
Live Action P.J. on Stage, 1970, No. 1153	.75	.175	
Lovin' You Barbie, 1983, No. 7072	.20	.100	
Magic Curl Barbie, black, 1982, No. 3989	.8	.25	

Barbie & Friends dolls

	MNB	MIB	Page #
Magic Curl Barbie, white, 1982, No. 3856	10	35	
Magic Moves Barbie, black, 1985, No. 3137	15	35	
Magic Moves Barbie, white, 1985, No. 2126	15	35	
Malibu Barbie, 1971, No. 1067	15	60	7, 100-101
Malibu Barbie (Sunset), 1975, No. 1067	15	40	
Malibu Christie, 1975, No. 7745	10	40	
Malibu Francie, 1971, No. 1068	15	45	
Malibu Ken, 1976, No. 1088	8	25	
Malibu P.J., 1975, No. 1087	5	45	
Malibu Skipper, 1977, No. 1069	8	45	
Midge, bendable leg, blond, brunette, titian, 1965, No. 1080	250	425	56
Midge, straight leg, blond, brunette, titian, 1963, No. 860	65	175	55
Miss Barbie (sleep eyes), 1964, No. 1060	400	1,200	42-43
Mod Hair Ken, 1972, No. 4224	45	65	114-115
Music Lovin' Barbie, 1985, No. 9988	15	45	
Music Lovin' Ken, 1985, No. 2388	15	45	
Music Lovin' Skipper, 1985, No. 2854	20	75	
My First Barbie, 1991, No. 9942	3	25	
My First Barbie, aqua and yellow dress, 1981, No. 1875	10	30	
My First Barbie, black, 1990, No. 9943	5	25	
My First Barbie, Hispanic, 1991, No. 9944	3	20	
My First Barbie, pink checkered dress, 1983, No. 1875	5	35	
My First Barbie, pink tutu, black, 1987, No. 1801	5	20	
My First Barbie, pink tutu, white, 1987, No. 1788	5	20	
My First Barbie, white, 1990, No. 9942	4	20	
My First Barbie, white dress, black, 1984, No. 9858	7	25	
My First Barbie, white dress, white, 1984, No. 1875	5	30	
My First Barbie, white tutu, black, 1988, No. 1281	6	15	
My First Barbie, white tutu, Hispanic, 1988, No. 1282	6	20	
My First Barbie, white tutu, white, 1988, No. 1280	5	20	
My First Ken, 1st issue, 1989, No. 1389	4	15	
My First Ken, Prince, 1990, No. 9940	4	15	
New Good Lookin' Ken, 1970, No. 1124	75	150	
New Look Ken, 1976, No. 9342	23	65	
Newport Barbie, two versions, 1974, No. 7807	25	140	
Nurse Whitney, 1987, No. 4405	20	45	
Ocean Friends Barbie, 1996, No. 15430	5	17	
Ocean Friends Ken, 1996, No. 15430	5	17	
Ocean Friends Kira, 1996, No. 15431	5	17	
Olympic Gymnast, blond, 1996, No. 15123	10	25	
P.J., talking, 1970, No. 1113	65	250	18, 52
P.J., Twist N Turn, 1970, No. 1118	125	300	
Party Treats Barbie, 1989, No. 4885	8	25	
Peaches n' Cream Barbie, black, 1984, No. 9516	8	40	
Peaches n' Cream Barbie, white, 1984, No. 7926	8	45	

Barbie & Friends dolls

	MNB	MIB	Page #
Perfume Giving Ken, black, 1989, No. 4555	6	25	
Perfume Giving Ken, white, 1989, No. 4554	6	25	
Perfume Pretty Barbie, black, 1989, No. 4552	8	25	
Perfume Pretty Barbie, white, 1989, No. 4551	8	25	
Perfume Pretty Whitney, 1987, No. 4557	8	35	
Pink n' Pretty Barbie, 1982, No. 3551	12	45	
Pink n' Pretty Christie, 1982, No. 3554	10	40	
Playtime Barbie, 1984, No. 5336	15	20	

Ponytail Dolls

	MNB	MIB	Page #
Ponytail Barbie #1, blond, 1959, No. 850	4,000	7,500	
Ponytail Barbie #1, brunette, 1959, No. 850	5,000	9,000	19, 20, 72-73
Ponytail Barbie #2, blond, 1959, No. 850	3,500	7,000	15, 23
Ponytail Barbie #2, brunette, 1959, No. 850	4,000	7,000	
Ponytail Barbie #3, blond, 1960, No. 850	500	1,300	24-25, 87
Ponytail Barbie #3, brunette, 1960, No. 850	750	1,400	75
Ponytail Barbie #4, blond, 1960, No. 850	250	575	76
Ponytail Barbie #4, brunette, 1960, No. 850	350	400	81
Ponytail Barbie #5, blond, 1961, No. 850	175	400	29

Dolls of the World, Parisian, 1991, $60 MIB

Barbie & Friends dolls

Barbie & Friends dolls	MNB	MIB	Page #
Ponytail Barbie #5, brunette, 1961, No. 850	250	450	28
Ponytail Barbie #5, titian, 1961, No. 850	250	500	
Ponytail Barbie #6, blond, brunette, titian 1962, No. 850	150	400	
Ponytail Swirl Style Barbie, blond, brunette, titian, 1964, No. 850	350	625	40-41
Ponytail Swirl Style Barbie, platinum, 1964, No. 850	500	1,200	
Pose n' Play Skipper (packaged in baggie), 1973, No. 1117	20	55	
Pretty Changes Barbie, 1978, No. 2598	8	45	
Pretty Party Barbie, 1983, No. 7194	12	30	
Quick Curl Barbie, 1972, No. 4220	20	80	110-111
Quick Curl Cara, 1974, No. 7291	20	60	
Quick Curl Deluxe Barbie, 1976, No. 9217	20	95	
Quick Curl Deluxe Cara, 1976, No. 9219	20	80	
Quick Curl Deluxe P.J., 1976, No. 9218	20	50	
Quick Curl Deluxe Skipper, 1976, No. 9428	20	50	
Quick Curl Francie, 1972, No. 4222	20	55	
Quick Curl Kelley, 1972, No. 4221	20	75	
Quick Curl Miss America, blond, 1974, No. 8697	35	75	129
Quick Curl Miss America, brunette, 1973, No. 8697	45	175	
Quick Curl Skipper, 1974, No. 4223	20	50	
Ricky, 1965, No. 1090	55	160	
Rocker Barbie, 1st issue, 1986, No. 1140	7	40	161
Rocker Barbie, 2nd issue, 1987, No. 3055	7	25	
Rocker Dana, 1st issue, 1986, No. 1196	7	40	
Rocker Dana, 2nd issue, 1987, No. 3158	7	20	
Rocker Dee-Dee, 1st issue, 1986, No. 1141	7	30	
Rocker Dee-Dee, 2nd issue, 1987, No. 3160	7	20	
Rocker Derek, 1st issue, 1986, No. 2428	7	30	
Rocker Derek, 2nd issue, 1987, No. 3173	7	20	
Rocker Diva, 1st issue, 1986, No. 2427	7	30	
Rocker Diva, 2nd issue, 1987, No. 3159	7	20	
Rocker Ken, 1st issue, 1986, No. 3131	7	30	160-161
Rollerskating Barbie, 1980, No. 1880	8	60	
Rollerskating Ken, 1980, No. 1881	8	40	
Safari Barbie, 1983, No. 4973	8	30	
Scott, 1979, No. 1019	15	60	
Sea Lovin' Barbie, 1984, No. 9109	8	35	
Sea Lovin' Ken, 1984, No. 9110	8	30	
Secret Messages Barbie, white or black, 2000, No. 26422	7	15	
Sensations Barbie, 1987, No. 4931	5	12	
Sensations Becky, 1987, No. 4977	5	12	
Sensations Belinda, 1987, No. 4976	5	12	
Sensations Bobsy, 1987, No. 4967	5	12	
Sit 'n Style Barbie, 2000, No. 23421	7	15	

Barbie & Friends dolls

Barbie & Friends dolls	MNB	MIB	Page #
Ski Fun Barbie, 1991, No. 7511	6	15	
Ski Fun Ken, 1991, No. 7512	6	15	
Ski Fun Midge, 1991, No. 7513	6	25	
Skipper, bendable leg, brunette, blond, titian, 1965, No. 1030	65	250	61
Skipper, straight leg, brunette, blond, titian, 1964, No. 950	50	195	58-59
Skipper, straight leg, reissues, brunette, blond, titian, 1971, No. 950	125	400	
Skipper, Twist N Turn, blond or brunette, curl pigtails, 1969, No. 1105	95	350	
Skipper, Twist N Turn, blond, brunette, redhead, long straight hair, 1968, No. 1105	95	350	
Skooter, bendable leg, brunette, blond, titian, 1966, No. 1120	100	350	66-67
Skooter, straight leg, brunette, blond, titian, 1965, No. 1040	55	180	64-65
Snowboard Barbie, 1996, No. 15408	10	20	
Sparkle Barbie, 1996, No. 15419	10	20	
Sport n' Shave Ken, 1980, No. 1294	8	40	
Stacey, talking, blond or redhead, side ponytail, 1968, No. 1125	175	475	
Stacey, Twist and Turn, blond or redhead, long ponytail with spit curls, 1968, No. 1165	150	475	
Stacey, Twist N Turn, blond or redhead, short rolled flip, 1969, No. 1165	175	475	
Standard Barbie, blond, brunette, long straight hair with bangs, 1967, No. 1190	250	550	
Standard Barbie, centered eyes, 1971, No. 1190	350	700	
Standard Barbie, titian, long straight hair with bangs, 1967, No. 1190	300	600	

Allan doll, straight leg, 1964, $125 MIB

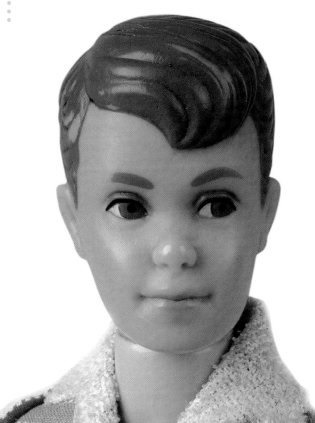

Barbie & Friends dolls

	MNB	MIB	Page #

Stars 'n Stripes
Air Force Barbie, 1990, No. 3360 .....15 ......50 — *131*
Air Force Ken, white or black, 1994, No. 11554/11555 ....15 25
Air Force Thunderbirds Barbie, white or black, 1994, No. 11552/11553 ....15 25
Army Barbie, white or black, 1993, No. 1234/5618 ....10 ......40 — *135*
Army Ken, white or black, 1993, No. 1237/5619 ....15 ......30 — *134*
Marine Corps Barbie, white or black, 1992, No. 7549/7594 ....10 ......35 — *135*
Marine Corps Ken, black or white, 1992, No. 5352/7574 ....20 ......40 — *135*
Navy Barbie, white or black, 1991, No. 9693/9694 ....10 ......35 — *124*

Style Magic Barbie, 1989, No. 1283 .....5 20
Style Magic Christie, 1989, No. 1288 ....5 20
Style Magic Skipper, 1989, No. 1915 ...10 20
Style Magic Whitney, 1989, No. 1290 ...5 20
Summit Barbie, Asian, 1990, No. 7029 .10 25
Summit Barbie, black, 1990, No. 7028 .12 25
Summit Barbie, Hispanic, 1990, No. 7030 ....10 28
Summit Barbie, white, 1990, No. 7027 ...8 25
Sun Gold Malibu Barbie, black, 1983, No. 7745 ....5 15
Sun Gold Malibu Barbie, Hispanic, 1985, No. 4970 ....3 20
Sun Gold Malibu Barbie, white, 1983, No. 1067 ....5 15
Sun Gold Malibu Ken, black, 1983, No. 3849 ....3 15
Sun Gold Malibu Ken, Hispanic, 1985, No. 4971 ....3 20
Sun Gold Malibu Ken, white, 1983, No. 1088 ....3 15
Sun Gold Malibu P.J., 1983, No. 1187 ...5 15
Sun Gold Malibu Skipper, 1983, No. 1069 ....5 15
Sun Lovin'Malibu Barbie, 1978, No. 1067 ....5 20
Sun Lovin'Malibu Ken, 1978, No. 1088 ..5 20
Sun Lovin'Malibu P.J., 1978, No. 1187 ..5 20
Sun Lovin'Malibu Skipper, 1978, No. 1069 ....5 20
Sun Valley Barbie, 1974, No. 7806 ....20 130
Sun Valley Ken, 1974, No. 7809 ......20 100
Sunsational Malibu Barbie, 1982, No. 1067 ....6 25
Sunsational Malibu Barbie, Hispanic, 1982, No. 4970 ....8 25
Sunsational Malibu Christie, 1982, No. 7745 ....6 20
Sunsational Malibu Ken, black, 1981, No. 3849 ....15 ......35 — *158-159*
Sunsational Malibu P.J., 1982, No. 1187 ..6 30
Sunsational Malibu Skipper, 1982, No. 1069 ....5 35
Sunset Malibu Christie, 1973, No. 7745 .20 65
Sunset Malibu Francie, 1971, No. 1068 .25 65
Sunset Malibu Ken, 1972, No. 1088 ...15 50
Sunset Malibu P.J., 1971, No. 1187 ....10 50
Sunset Malibu Skipper, 1971, No. 1069 .20 50

Barbie & Friends dolls

	MNB	MIB	Page #

Super Hair Barbie, black, 1987, No. 3296 ....8 20
Super Hair Barbie, white, 1987, No. 3101 ....8 25
Super Sport Ken, 1982, No. 5839 ......8 20
Super Talk Barbie, 1994, No. 12290 ...10 20
Super Teen Skipper, 1978, No. 2756 ....7 20
Supersize Barbie, 1977, No. 9828 .....75 .....200 — *120-121*
Supersize Bride Barbie, 1977, No. 9975 ....150 295
Supersize Christie, 1977, No. 9839 ....75 275
Supersize Super Hair Barbie, 1979, No. 2844 ....85 175
Superstar Ballerina Barbie, 1976, No. 4983 ....20 60
Superstar Barbie, 1977, No. 9720 .....15 ......70 — *122-123*
Superstar Barbie, 1988, No. 1604 .....45 95
Superstar Barbie 30th Anniversary, black, 1989, No. 1605 ....6 35
Superstar Barbie 30th Anniversary, white, 1989, No. 1604 ....8 25
Superstar Christie, 1977, No. 9950 ....20 75
Superstar Ken, 1978, No. 2211 ....17 75
Superstar Ken, black, 1989, No. 1550 ...5 30
Superstar Ken, white, 1989, No. 1535 ...7 50
Superstar Malibu Barbie, 1977, No. 1067 ....10 35
Sweet 16 Barbie, 1974, No. 7796 ......25 .....125 — *118-119*
Sweet Roses P.J., 1983, No. 7455 ......15 25
Swimming Champion Barbie, 2000, No. 24590 ....7 15
Talk With Me Barbie, 1997, No. 17350 .25 50
Talking Barbie, chignon with nape curls, blond, brunette, titian, 1970, No. 1115 ....200 500
Talking Barbie, side ponytail with spit curls, blond or brunette, 1968, No. 1115 ....150 .....425 — *50-51*
Talking Busy Barbie, 1972, No. 1195 ..125 .....300 — *105*
Talking Busy Ken, 1972, No. 1196 ....80 160
Talking Busy Steffie, 1972, No. 1186 ..175 .....350 — *88*
Talking Ken, 1969, No. 1111 ....75 175
Teacher Barbie, painted on panties, black, 1996, No. 13915 ....15 20
Teacher Barbie, painted on panties, white, 1996, No. 13914 ....15 25
Teacher Barbie, w/out panties, white, 1995, No. 13914 ....25 ......50 — *170-171*
Teen Dance Jazzie, 1989, No. 3634 .....7 35
Teen Fun Skipper Cheerleader, 1987, No. 5893 ....5 15
Teen Fun Skipper Party Teen, 1987, No. 5899 ....5 15
Teen Fun Skipper Workout, 1987, No. 5889 ....5 15
Teen Jazzie (Teen Dance), 1989, No. 3634 ....4 35
Teen Looks Jazzie Cheerleader, 1989, No. 3631 ....4 20
Teen Looks Jazzie Workout, 1989, No. 3633 ....4 20
Teen Scene Jazzie, two box versions, 1991, No. 5507 ....5 35
Teen Sweetheart Skipper, 1988, No. 4855 ....5 25
Teen Talk Barbie, 1992, No. 5745 .....15 45
Teen Talk Barbie, "Math is Tough" variation, 1992, No. 5745 ....50 .....275 — *164-165*
Teen Time Courtney, 1988, No. 1950 ....5 10

**Talking Christie,
1968, $200 MIB**

priceguide

<table>
<tr><td>

Collector Editions & Store Exclusives</td><td>MNB</td><td>MIB</td><td>Page #</td></tr>
</table>

Artist Series

Reflections of Light Barbie, Renoir, 1999, No. 23884 .... 40 80
Sunflower Barbie, Van Gogh, 1998, No. 19366 .... 40 80
Water Lily Barbie, Monet, 1997, No. 17783 .... 50 110

Avon

Blushing Bride Barbie, white or black, 2000 .... 10 25
Fruit Fantasy Barbie, blond, 1999 ..... 10 25
Fruit Fantasy Barbie, brunette, 1999 ... 15 30
Lemon-Lime Barbie, 1999, No. 20318 .. 10 25
Mrs. P.F.E. Albee, 1997, No. 17690 .... 22 65
Mrs. P.F.E. Albee #2, 1998, No. 20330 . 30 75
Representative Barbie, black, white, Hispanic, 1999 .... 20 50
Snow Sensation, black or white, 1999 . 15 40
Spring Blossom, black, 1996, No. 15202 .... 10 20
Spring Blossom, white, 1996, No. 15201 .... 10 25
Spring Petals Barbie, black, 1997, No. 16871 .... 15 30
Spring Petals Barbie, blond or brunette, 1997, No. 10746/16872 .... 15 30
Spring Tea Party Barbie, black 15 30
Spring Tea Party Barbie, blond or brunette, No. 18658 ..... 15 30
Strawberry Sorbet Barbie, 1999, No. 20317 .... 10 25
Timeless Silhouette Barbie, white or black, 2001 .... 10 25
Victorian Skater Barbie, white or black, 2000 .... 10 35
Winter Rhapsody Barbie, black, No. 16354 .... 15 30
Winter Rhapsody Barbie, blond or brunette, No. 16353/16873 ...... 15 30
Winter Splendor Barbie, black, 1998, No. 19358 .... 20 40
Winter Splendor Barbie, white, 1998, No. 19357 .... 15 35
Winter Velvet, black, 1996, No. 15587 . 10 85
Winter Velvet, white, 1996, No. 15571 . 17 75

B Mine Barbie, 1993, No. 11182 .... 7 25
Back To School, 1993, No. 3208 ..... 15 35
Back to School, 1997 .... 5 10
Ballerina Dreams Barbie, 2000, No. 20676 .... 5 12
Ballerina on Tour Gift Set, 1976, No. 9613 .... 25 125
Ballet Lessons Barbie, black or white, 2000 .... 5 12
Ballroom Beauties, Midnight Waltz, 1996, No. 15685 .... 35 85

Ballroom Beauties, Moonlight Waltz Barbie, 1997, No. 17763 ..... 40 80
Ballroom Beauties, Starlight Waltz Barbie, 1995, No. 14070 .... 35 85

<table>
<tr><td>

Collector Editions & Store Exclusives</td><td>MNB</td><td>MIB</td><td>Page #</td></tr>
</table>

Barbie 2000, white or black, 2000, No. 27409/27410 .... 30 59
Barbie 2001, black, 2001, No. 50842 .. 15 50
Barbie 2001, white, 2001, No. 50841 ... 15 50
Barbie and Friends: Ken, Barbie, P.J., 1983, No. 4431 .... 25 75
Barbie and Ken Camping Out, 1983 ... 25 65
Barbie and Ken Tennis Gift Set, 1962, No. 892 .... 450 1,000
Barbie and Krissy Magical Mermaids, black or white, 2000 .... 15 30
Barbie Beautiful Blues Gift Set, 1967, No. 3303 .... 1,600 ... 3,000

Barbie Collector's Club

Café Society, 1998, No. 18892 .... 50 200
Club Couture, 2000, No. 26068 ..... 25 65
Embassy Waltz, 1999, No. 23386 ..... 45 150
Grand Premiere, 1997, No. 16498 .... 100 225
Holiday Treasures 1999, 1999 ...... 100 250
Holiday Treasures 2000, 2000, No. 27673 .... 35 75
Midnight Tuxedo, white or black, 2001 .... 25 65

Barbie Millicent Roberts Matinee Today, 1996, No. 16079 .... 22 60
Barbie Millicent Roberts Perfectly Suited, 1997, No. 17567 .... 30 45
Barbie Millicent Roberts Pinstripe Power, 1998, No. 19791 .... 30 50
Barbie's Round the Clock Gift Set, Bubblecut, 1964, No. 1013 .... 1,200 3,000
Barbie's Sparkling Pink Gift Set, Bubblecut, 1964, No. 1011 .... 1,000 2,400
Barbie's Wedding Party Gift Set, 1964, No. 1017 .... 1,000 2,400
Beauty Secrets Barbie Pretty Reflections Gift Set, 1979, No. 1702 .... 40 100
Best Buy Detective Barbie, 2000, No. 24189 .... 8 17
Bill Blass Barbie, 1997, No. 17040 .... 35 75
Billions of Dreams Barbie, 1997, No. 17641 .... 150 ..... 350 *194-195*
Billy Boy Feelin' Groovy Barbie, 1986, No. 3421 .... 100 175
Billy Boy Le Nouveau Theatre de la Mode Barbie, 1985, No. 6279 . 100 200

Birds of Beauty

#1 Peacock Barbie, 1998, No. 19365 .. 32 70
#2 Flamingo Barbie, 1999, No. 22957 . 50 100
#3 Swan Barbie, 2000, No. 27682 ..... 40 80

Birthday Fun at McDonald's Gift Set, 1994, No. 11589 .... 15 35

Birthday Wishes

#1, black or white, 1999, No. 21128/21509 .... 15 35
#2, black or white, 2000, No. 24667/24668 .... 20 40

Essence of Nature #1 Water Rhapsody, 1998, $90 MIB

Superstar Barbie
1977, $70 MIB

Collector Editions & Store Exclusives

	MNB	MIB	Page #
Rapunzel, 1995, No. 13016	.25	.50	
Sleeping Beauty, 1998	.20	.45	
Snow White, 1999, No. 21130	.20	.40	
Christian Dior 50th Anniversary, 1997, No. 16013	.35	.75	
Christian Dior Barbie, 1995, No. 13168	.60	.100	
Chuck E. Cheese Barbie, 1996, No. 14615	.15	.30	

City Seasons

	MNB	MIB	Page #
Autumn in London, 1999, No. 22257	.20	.50	
Autumn in Paris, 1998, No. 19367	.18	.50	203
Spring in Tokyo, 1999, No. 19430	.25	.50	201
Spring in Tokyo, Internet exclusive, 1999, No. 23499	.30	.65	
Summer in Rome, 1999, No. 19431	.25	.50	202
Winter in Montreal, 1999, No. 22258	.20	.50	200
Winter in New York, 1998, No. 19429	.18	.50	202

Classic Ballet

	MNB	MIB	Page #
Flower Ballerina, 2001, No. 28375	.10	.28	
Marzipan, 1999, No. 20581	.15	.30	172
Snowflake, 2000, No. 25642	.15	.30	
Sugar Plum Fairy, 1997, No. 17056	.15	.35	
Swan Lake, black or white, 1998, No. 18509/18510	.15	.30	

Classique

	MNB	MIB
Benefit Ball Barbie, 1992, No. 1521	.50	.125
City Style Barbie, 1993, No. 10149	.30	.100
Evening Extravaganza, 1994, No. 11622	.25	.65
Evening Extravaganza, black, 1994, No. 11638	.25	.75
Evening Sophisticate, 1998, No. 19361	.18	.50
Midnight Gala, 1995, No. 12999	.25	.70
Opening Night Barbie, 1993, No. 10148	.30	.95
Romantic Interlude Barbie, 1997, No. 17136	.15	.45
Romantic Interlude Barbie, black, 1997, No. 17137	.15	.45
Starlight Dance, 1996, No. 15461	.20	.45
Starlight Dance, black, 1996, No. 15819	.20	.45
Uptown Chic Barbie, 1994, No. 11623	.25	.70

Coca-Cola

	MNB	MIB
Barbie #1, carhop, 1999, No. 22831	.20	.65
Barbie #2, 2000, No. 24637	.25	.60
Cheerleader, 2001	.15	.50
Disney Teddy & Doll Convention, brunette, limited to 1,500	.45	.95
Fashion Classic #1, Soda Fountain Sweetheart, 1996	.90	.150
Fashion Classic #2, After the Walk, 1997, No. 17341	.100	.200
Fashion Classic #3, Summer		

Collector Editions & Store Exclusives

	MNB	MIB	Page #
Daydreams, 1998, No. 19739	.50	.100	
Ken, 2000, No. 25678	.25	.60	
Party, 1999, No. 22964	.5	.15	
Picnic, 1998, No. 19626	.5	.15	
Splash, 2000, No. 22590	.5	.15	

Collectors' Request

	MNB	MIB	Page #
Commuter Set, 1999, No. 21510	.25	.50	
Sophisticated Lady, 1999, No. 24930	.25	.60	189
Suburban Shopper, 2000	.15	.45	
Twist N Turn Smasheroo, brunette, 1998, No. 18941	.25	.40	
Twist N'Turn Smasheroo, red hair, 1998, No. 23258	.25	.50	
Cool Collecting Barbie, 2000, No. 25525	.25	.60	

Couture Collection

	MNB	MIB
Portrait in Taffeta Barbie, 1996, No. 15528	.65	.150
Serenade in Satin Barbie, 1997, No. 17572	.65	.150
Symphony in Chiffon, 1998, No. 21295	.65	.150
Cracker Barrel Country Charm Barbie, 2001	.5	.15
Dance Club Barbie Gift Set, 1989, No. 4917	.25	.60
Dance Magic Gift Set Barbie & Ken, 1990, No. 5409	.15	.35
Dance Sensation Barbie Gift Set, 1984, No. 9058	.15	.40
Democratic National Convention Delegate Barbie, 2000	.25	.150
Empress Sissy, Barbie as, 1996, No. 15846	.35	.80

Enchanted Seasons

	MNB	MIB
#1 Snow Princess, 1994, No. 11875	.40	.125
#2 Spring Bouquet, 1995, No. 12989	.40	.125
#3 Autumn Glory, 1996, No. 15204	.40	.125
#4 Summer Splendor, 1997, No. 15683	.40	.125
Enchanted World of Fairies, Fairy of the Forest, 2000, No. 25639	.25	.49
Enchanted World of Fairies, Fairy of the Garden, 2001	.15	.45
Escada Barbie, 1996, No. 15948	.40	.70

Essence of Nature

	MNB	MIB
#1 Water Rhapsody, 1998, No. 19847	.40	.90
#2 Whispering Wind, 1999, No. 22834	.40	.80
#3 Dancing Fire, 2000, No. 26327	.35	.79

FAO Schwarz

American Beauty, Barbie as George

Collector Editions & Store Exclusives

Collector Editions & Store Exclusives

Malibu Ken, 1976, $25 MIB

Collector Editions & Store Exclusives

	MNB	MIB	Page #
blue box	.5	.15	
Grand Entrance Barbie,			
white or black, 2001	.25	.65	
Grand Ole Opry #1 Country Rose			
Barbie, 1997, No. 17782	.40	.80	
Grand Ole Opry #2 Rising Star Barbie,			
1998, No. 17864	.50	.100	
Grand Ole Opry Barbie and Kenny			
Country Duet,1999, No. 23498	.55	.100	

Great Eras

	MNB	MIB	Page #
#1, Gibson Girl, 1993, No. 3702	.25	.125	
#2, Flapper, 1993, No. 4063	.25	.175	
#3, Egyptian Queen, 1994, No. 11397	.20	.120	
#4, Southern Belle, 1994, No. 11478	.20	.100	
#5, Medieval Lady, 1995, No. 12791	.25	.60	
#6, Elizabethan Queen, 1995,			
No. 12792	.25	.60	
#7, Grecian Goddess, 1996, No. 15005	.35	.50	
#8, Victorian Lady, 1996, No. 14900	.35	.50	
#9, French Lady, 1997, No. 16707	.35	.50	
#10, Chinese Empress, 1997,			
No. 16708	.35	.50	

Great Fashions of the 20th Century

	MNB	MIB	Page #
#1, Promenade in the Park, 1998,			
No. 18630	.20	.65	
#2, Dance 'til Dawn, 1998, No. 19631	.30	.65	
#3, Steppin Out Barbie, 1999,			
No. 21531	.30	.60	
#4, Fabulous Forties, 2000, No. 22162	.25	.60	
#5, Nifty Fifties, 2000, No. 27675	.25	.60	
#6, Groovy Sixties, 2000, No. 27676	.25	.60	204-205
#7, Peace & Love 70s Barbie,			
2000, No. 27677	.15	.50	

	MNB	MIB	Page #
Groliers Book Club The Front Window Barbie,			
2000, No. 27968	.10	.35	

Hallmark

	MNB	MIB	Page #
Fair Valentine Barbie, 1998	.20	.45	
Gold Crown #1, Victorian Elegance			
Barbie, 1994, No. 12579	.75	.80	
Gold Crown #2, Holiday Memories			
Barbie, 1995, No. 14108	.20	.50	
Holiday Sensation Barbie,			
1999, No. 19792	.15	.50	
Holiday Traditions Barbie,			
1997, No. 17094	.25	.50	
Holiday Voyage Barbie, 1998	.25	.60	
Sentimental Valentine Barbie, 1997	.23	.50	
Sweet Valentine Barbie,			
1996, No. 14880	.20	.60	
Yuletide Romance Barbie,			
1996, No. 15621	.20	.50	

	MNB	MIB	Page #
Hanae Mori Barbie, 2000	.50	.99	
Happy Birthday Barbie Gift Set,			
1985	.20	.40	

Collector Editions & Store Exclusives

Happy Holidays

	MNB	MIB	Page #
#1, 1988, No. 1703	.75	.700	148
#2, 1989, No. 3253	.50	.175	148
#3, 1990, No. 4098	.25	.110	148
1990, black, No. 4543	.20	.85	
#4, 1991, No. 1871	.40	.150	149
1991, black, No. 2696	.40	.100	
#5, 1992, No. 1429	.30	.120	149
1992, black, No. 2396	.30	.80	
#6, 1993, No. 10824	.30	.95	149
1993, black, No. 10911	.30	.60	
#7, 1994, No. 12155	.30	.120	
1994, black, No. 12156	.30	.75	150
#8, 1995, No. 14123	.20	.65	150
1995, black, No. 14124	.20	.55	
#9, 1996, white or black, No. 15646	.30	.55	150
#10, 1997, No. 17832	.5	.25	150
1997, black, No. 17833	.5	.25	
#11, 1998, white or black,			
No. 20200/20201	.10	.25	151

	MNB	MIB	Page #
Harrods/Hamleys West End Barbie,			
1996, No. 17590	.20	.75	
Harvey Nichols Special Edition			
(limited to 250), 1995, No. 0175	.500	.900	
Hawaiian Barbie, 1982, No. 7470	.25	.100	
Hills Blue Elegance Barbie,			
1992, No. 1879	.12	.40	
Hills Evening Sparkle, 1990, No. 3274	.10	.35	
Hills Moonlight Rose, 1991, No. 3549	.7	.30	
Hills Party Lace Barbie, 1989,			
No. 4843	.15	.35	
Hills Polly Pocket Barbie,			
1994, No. 12412	.12	.25	
Hills Sea Pearl Mermaid Barbie,			
1995, No. 13940	.8	.35	
Hills Sidewalk Chalk Barbie,			
1998, No. 19784	.10	.25	
Hills Teddy Fun Barbie,			
1996, No. 15684	.10	.25	
Holiday Angel #1, black,			
2000, No. 28080	.20	.50	
Holiday Angel #1, white,			
2000, No. 26914	.20	.50	
Holiday Angel #2, black,			
2001, No. 29770	.15	.45	
Holiday Angel #2, white,			
2001, No. 29769	.15	.45	
Holiday Dreams Barbie,			
1994, No. 12192	.10	.20	
Holiday Hostess Barbie,			
1993, No. 10280	.25	.50	
Holiday Season, 1996, No. 15581	.5	.15	
Holiday Singing Sisters Gift Set, 2000	.15	.50	
Holiday Surprise Barbie,			
white or black, 2000	.5	.15	
Holiday Treats Barbie, 1997	.5	.12	
Hollywood Hair Deluxe Gift Set,			
1993, No. 10928	.15	.35	

Hollywood Legends

	MNB	MIB	Page #
Dorothy (*Wizard of Oz*),			
1995, No. 12701	.20	.180	

Collector Editions & Store Exclusives

	MNB	MIB	Page #
Eliza Doolittle (*My Fair Lady*), green coat, 1996, No. 15498	30	65	
Eliza Doolittle (*My Fair Lady*), lace ball gown, 1996, No. 15500	30	95	
Eliza Doolittle (*My Fair Lady*), pink, 1996, No. 15501	30	75	
Eliza Doolittle (*My Fair Lady*), white lace gown w/parasol, 1996, No. 15497	30	75	
Glinda (*Wizard of Oz*), 1996, No. 14901	35	75	
Ken as Cowardly Lion (*Wizard of Oz*), 1996, No. 16573	35	75	
Ken as Henry Higgins (*My Fair Lady*), 1996, No. 15499	25	65	
Ken as Rhett Butler, 1994, No. 12741	25	65	
Ken as Scarecrow (*Wizard of Oz*), 1996, No. 16497	35	65	
Ken as Tin Man (*Wizard of Oz*), 1996, No. 14902	35	65	
Maria (*Sound of Music*), 1995, No. 13676	20	50	
Marilyn Monroe, pink, 1997, No. 17451	20	45	
Marilyn Monroe, red, 1997, No. 17452	20	45	
Marilyn Monroe, white, 1997, No. 17155	20	45	
Scarlett O'Hara, black/white dress, 1993, No. 13254	25	70	
Scarlett O'Hara, green velvet curtain, 1994, No. 12045	25	70	
Scarlett O'Hara, green/white silk dress, 1995, No. 12997	25	65	
Scarlett O'Hara, red velvet dress, 1994, No. 12815	25	70	

Day-To-Night Ken, 1984, $20 MIB

Collector Editions & Store Exclusives

	MNB	MIB	Page #
Hollywood Movie Star			
Between Takes, 2000, No. 27684	25	50	
By the Pool, 2000, No. 27684	25	50	
Day in the Sun, 2000, No. 2000	25	50	
Hollywood Cast Party, 2001, No. 50825	15	45	
Hollywood Premiere, 2000, No. 26914	25	50	
Publicity Tour, 2001	15	45	
Home Shopping Club Evening Flame, 1991, No. 1865	70	125	
Home Shopping Club Golden Allure Barbie, 1999	5	30	
Home Shopping Club Premiere Night, 1999	5	30	
Japanese Living Eli, 1970	700	1,400	
JCPenney			
Enchanted Evening, 1991, No. 2702	40	70	
Evening Elegance, 1990, No. 7057	40	60	
Evening Enchantment, 1998, No. 19783	25	65	
Evening Majesty, 1997, No. 17235	10	25	
Evening Sensation, 1992, No. 1278	12	55	
Golden Winter, 1993, No. 10684	12	55	
Night Dazzle, 1994, No. 12191	15	55	
Original Arizona Jean Co. Barbie #1, 1996, No. 15441	12	28	
Original Arizona Jean Co. Barbie #2, 1997, No. 18020	12	25	
Original Arizona Jean Co. Barbie #3, 1998, No. 19873	12	25	
Royal Enchantment, 1995, No. 14010	25	40	
Winter Renaissance, 1996, No. 15570	10	25	
JCPenney/Sears Evening Recital Barbie, Stacie, Kelly and Tommy, 2000, No. 27954	15	45	
Jubilee Series			
Crystal Jubilee, limited to 20,000, 1999, No. 21923	150	325	
Gold Jubilee, limited to 5,000, 1994, No. 12009	300	750	
Pink Jubilee, limited to 1,200, 1989, No. 3756	800	2,200	
Julia Simply Wow Gift Set, 1969	400	1,500	
K-B Fantasy Ball Barbie, 1997, No. 18594	10	20	
K-B Fashion Avenue Barbie, 1998, No. 20782	8	15	
K-B Glamour Barbie, black, 1997	10	20	
K-B Starlight Carousel Barbie, 1998, No. 19708	10	20	
Keepsake Treasures, Barbie and Curious George, 2001	15	30	
Keepsake Treasures, Barbie and the Tale of Peter Rabbit, 1998, No. 19360	15	40	
Kissing Barbie Gift Set, 1978, No. 2977	25	65	

Collector Editions & Store Exclusives

	MNB	MIB	Page #

Kmart

	MNB	MIB	Page #
March of Dimes Walk America Barbie & Kelly Gift Set, 1999, No. 20843	15	25	
March of Dimes Walk America Barbie, black or white, 1998, No. 18506/18507	10	25	
Peach Pretty Barbie, 1989, No. 4870	10	30	
Pretty in Purple, black, 1992, No. 3121	12	25	
Pretty in Purple, white, 1992, No. 3117	12	25	
Route 66 Barbecue Bash, 2000	8	25	
Very Berry Barbie, white or black, 2000	5	10	

	MNB	MIB	Page #
Kool-Aid Barbie, 1996	15	40	
Kool-Aid Wacky Warehouse Barbie I, 1993, No. 10309	25	60	
Kool-Aid Wacky Warehouse Barbie II, 1994, No. 11763	25	50	
Kraft Treasures Barbie, 1992	30	55	
L.E. Festival Holiday Barbie (540 made), 1994	700	1,200	
Life Ball Barbie #1, Vivienne Westwood, 1998	200	500	
Life Ball Barbie #2, Christian LaCroix, 1999	200	500	
Little Debbie #1, 1993, No. 10123	25	60	
Little Debbie #2, 1996, No. 14616	15	30	
Little Debbie #3, 1998, No. 16352	15	25	
Little Debbie #4, 1999, No. 24977	10	25	
Living Barbie Action Accents Gift Set, 1970, No. 1585	500	1,500	
Loving You Barbie Gift Set, 1983, No. 7583	45	100	

	MNB	MIB	Page #
Macy's Anne Klein Barbie, 1997, No. 17603	30	70	
Macy's City Shopper, Nicole Miller, 1996, No. 16289	25	70	
Magic & Mystery, Morgan LeFay and Merlin, 2000, No. 27287	50	100	
Magic & Mystery, Tales of the Arabian Nights, 2001, No. 50827	40	90	
Major League Baseball Chicago Cubs, 1999, No. 23883	20	45	
Major League Baseball Los Angeles Dodgers, 1999, No. 23882	20	45	
Major League Baseball New York Yankees, 1999, No. 23881	20	45	
Make-A-Valentine Barbie, white or black, 1999	5	15	
Malibu Barbie "The Beach Party," w/case, 1979, No. 1703	17	35	
Malibu Ken Surf's Up Gift Set, 1971, No. 1248	75	200	

Masquerade Gala

	MNB	MIB	Page #
#1, Illusion, 1997, No. 18667	50	120	
#2, Rendezvous, 1998, No. 20647	50	85	
#3, Venetian Opulence, 2000, No. 24501	50	100	

Mattel Festival

	MNB	MIB	Page #
35th Anniversary (3,500 made), 1994	250	200	
35th Anniversary Gift Set (975 made),			

Collector Editions & Store Exclusives

	MNB	MIB	Page #
1994, No. 11591	400	550	
Banquet, blond, 1994	175	225	
Banquet, brunette, 1994	125	250	
Banquet, redhead, 1994	225	225	
Doctor, brunette (1,500 made), 1994, No. 11160	75	100	
Gymnast (1,500 made), 1994, No. 11921	75	80	
Happy Holiday, 1994, No. 12155	270	1,200	
Haute Couture, rainbow (500 made), 1994	200	300	
Haute Couture, red velvet (480 made), 1994	200	375	
Night Dazzle, brunette (420 made), 1994, No. 12191	150	400	
Snow Princess, brunette (285 made), 1994, No. 12905	600	1,250	

	MNB	MIB	Page #
Meijers Hula Hoop, 1997, No. 18167	10	20	
Meijers Ice Cream, 1998, No. 19820	10	20	
Meijers Ladybug Fun, 1997, No. 17695	10	20	
Meijers Shopping Fun, 1993, No. 10051	10	20	
Meijers Something Extra, 1992, No. 0863	10	20	
Mervyns Ballerina Barbie, 1983, No. 4983	30	75	
Mervyns Fabulous Fur, 1986, No. 7093	25	65	
Midge's Ensemble Gift Set, 1964, No. 1012	1,200	3,150	
Millennium Bride, limited to 10,000, 1999, No. 24505	150	300	
Mix n'Match Gift Set, 1962, No. 857	800	1,850	
Montgomery Ward (mail order box), 1972, No. 3210	30	700	
Montgomery Ward Barbie (pink box), 1972, No. 3210	350	800	*112-113*
My First Barbie Gift Set, 1991, No. 2483	8	20	
My First Barbie Gift Set, pink tutu, 1986, No. 1979	15	35	
My First Barbie Gift Set, pink tutu, 1987, No. 5386	18	40	
My First Barbie, pink tutu, Zayre's Hispanic, 1987, No. 1875	8	45	
NASCAR Barbie #1, Kyle Petty #44, 1998, No. 20442	20	25	
NASCAR Barbie #2, Bill Elliott #94, 1999, No. 22954	20	45	

National Convention

	MNB	MIB	Page #
A Date with Barbie Doll in Atlanta, 1998	100	350	
Barbie and the Bandstand, 1996	225	450	
Barbie Around the World Festival, 1985	125	300	
Barbie Convention 1980, 1980	125	350	
Barbie Forever Young, 1989	125	300	
Barbie in the Old West, 2000	85	225	
Barbie Loves a Fairytale, 1991	150	250	
Barbie Loves New York, 1984	125	275	
Barbie Ole, 1995	225	400	
Barbie Wedding Dreams, 1992	50	200	
Barbie's Pow Wow, 1983	125	350	
Barbie's Reunion, 1986	125	275	

Quick Curl Barbie
1972, $80 MIB

Collector Editions & Store Exclusives

Nostalgic Reproductions

Stars 'n Stripes, Marine Corps Barbie, 1992, $35 MIB

Collector Editions & Store Exclusives

Pop Culture Series

Collector Editions & Store Exclusives

	MNB	MIB	Page #

Red Romance Barbie,
1993, No. 3161 . . . . .7 15
Republican National Convention
Delegate Barbie, 2000 . . . . .25 150
Romantic Bride Barbie, black,
2001, No. 29439 . . . . .15 45
Romantic Bride Barbie, blond,
2001, No. 29438 . . . . , , , .15 45

Royal Jewels
Countess of Rubies, 2001 . . . . .40 100
Duchess of Diamonds, 2001 . . . . .40 100
Empress of Emeralds, 2000,
No. 25680 . . . . .50 100
Queen of Sapphires, 2000, No. 24924 . .50 100

Russell Stover Easter, 1996, No. 14956 .10 25
Russell Stover Easter, 1997, No. 17091 . .5 15
Russell Stover Easter (w/Easter basket),
1996, No. 14617 . . . . .10 25

Sam's Club
50s Fun Barbie, 1996, No. 15820 . . . . .20 40
60s Fun Barbie, blond, 1997,
No. 17252 . . . . .15 25
60s Fun Barbie, red hair,
1997, No. 17693 . . . . .10 30
70s Fun Barbie, blond, 1998,
No. 19928 . . . . .12 25
70s Fun Barbie, brunette,
1998, No. 19929 . . . . .15 30
Barbie Sisters' Celebration,
Barbie and Krissy, 2000 . . . . .10 25
Bronze Sensation Barbie,
1998, No. 20022 . . . . .25 75
Dinner Date Barbie, blond,
1998, No. 19016 . . . . .8 15
Dinner Date Barbie, red hair,
1998, No. 19037 . . . . .9 20
Festiva Barbie, 1993, No. 10339 . . . . . .15 35
Jewel Jubilee Barbie, 1991, No. 2366 . .25 60
Party Sensation Barbie, 1990, No. 9025 .20 50
Peach Blossom Barbie, 1992, No. 7009 .20 40
Season's Greetings Barbie,
1994, No. 12384 . . . . .25 60
Sweet Moments Barbie,
1997, No. 17642 . . . . .12 20
Wedding Fantasy Barbie Gift Set,
1993, No. 10924 . . . . .30 70
Winter Fantasy Barbie, blond or
brunette, 1997, No. 17249/17666 .10 20
Winter's Eve Barbie, 1995, No. 13613 . .12 28

School Spirit Barbie, 1996 . . . . .5 10
Schooltime Barbie 1995, 1995 . . . . . . .5 10
Schooltime Barbie 1998, 1998 . . . . . . .5 10

Sears
100th Celebration Barbie,
1986, No. 2998 . . . . .20 75
Barbie Twinkle Town Set,
1969, No. 1866 . . . . .800 1,600

Collector Editions & Store Exclusives

	MNB	MIB	Page #

Blossom Beautiful Barbie,
1992, No. 3817 . . . . .100 275
Blue Starlight, 1997, No. 17125 . . . . . . .15 30
Dream Princess, 1992, No. 2306 . . . . . .25 50
Enchanted Princess, 1993, No. 10292 . .35 60
Evening Enchantment, 1989, No. 3596 .10 40
Evening Flame, 1996, No. 15533 . . . . . .15 30
Lavender Surprise, 1990, No. 9049 . . . . .8 35
Lavender Surprise, black, 1990,
No. 5588 . . . . .8 30
Lilac and Lovely Barbie, 1988,
No. 7669 . . . . .10 45
Perfectly Plaid Gift Set, 1971,
No. 1193 . . . . .800 1,500
Pink Reflections, 1998, No. 19130 . . . .10 25
Ribbons and Roses Barbie,
1995, No. 13011 . . . . .10 50
Silver Sweetheart Barbie,
1994, No. 12410 . . . . .17 50
Skooter Cut n' Button Gift Set,
1967, No. 1036 . . . . .150 650
Southern Belle, 1991, No. 2586 . . . . . .10 40
Star Dream Barbie, 1987, No. 4550 . . . .10 60
Winter Sports, 1975, No. 9042 . . . . . . .65 115

Secret Hearts Gift Set, 1993,
No. 10929 . . . . .17 35
See's Candy Barbie, white or
black, 2000 . . . . .15 45

Service Merchandise
Blue Rhapsody, 1991, No. 1364 . . . . . .125 175
City Sophisticate, 1994, No. 12005 . . . .20 85
Definitely Diamonds, 1998, No. 20204 .45 110
Dream Bride, black or white,

Stars 'n Stripes Army Barbie and Ken dolls, 1993, $30 to $40 MIB each

Collector Editions & Store Exclusives

	MNB	MIB	Page #

1997, No. 17933/17153 . . . . .10 25
Evening Symphony, 1998, No. 19777 . . .10 25
Ruby Romance, 1995, No. 13612 . . . . .25 50
Satin Nights, two earring versions,
    1992, No. 1886 . . . . .20 80
Sea Princess, 1996, No. 15531 . . . . . .15 30
Sparkling Splendor, 1993, No. 10994 . . .17 50

Sharin Sisters Gift Set, 1992, No. 5716 .12 25
Sharin Sisters Gift Set, 1993, No. 10143 12 25
Shopko/Venture Blossom Beauty,
    1991, No. 3142 . . . . .10 40
Shopko/Venture Party Perfect,
    1992, No. 1876 . . . . .12 35
Skipper Party Time Gift Set,
    1964, No. 1021 . . . . .100 550
Skipper Swing 'a'Rounder Gym Gift Set,
    1972, No. 1172 . . . . .100 400
Snap 'N Play Gift Set (Snap 'N Play
    Deluxe), 1992, No. 2262 . . . . . . .12 35
Society Hound Barbie, 2001 . . . . .30 80

Spiegel
Golden Qi-Pao Barbie, 1998,
    No. 20866 . . . . .30 65
Regal Reflections, 1992, No. 4116 . . . . .75 275
Royal Invitation, 1993, No. 10969 . . . . .35 100
Shopping Chic, 1995, No. 14009 . . . . . .35 75
Sterling Wishes, 1991, No. 3347 . . . . . .45 130
Summer Sophisticate, 1996, No. 15591 .20 45
Theatre Elegance, 1994, No. 12077 . . .150 180
Winner's Circle, 1997, No. 17441 . . . . .35 50

Splash 'N Color Barbie Gift Set, 1997 . .10 20
Spring Bouquet Barbie, 1993, No. 3477 .10 20
Spring Parade Barbie, 1992, No. 7008 . .15 25
Spring Parade Barbie, black,
    1992, No. 2257 . . . . .15 25

Storybook Favorites
Goldilocks and the Three Bears (Kelly),
    2001, No. 29605 . . . . .8 20
Hansel & Gretel (Kelly and Tommy),
    2000, No. 28535 . . . . .5 17
Raggedy Ann and Andy (Kelly and
    Tommy), 2000, No. 24639 . . . . . . .5 17

Sweet Spring Barbie, 1992, No. 3208 . . .10 20
Sydney 2000 Olympic Pin Collector,
    black or white, 2000,
    No. 25644/26302 . . . . .20 40

Target
35th Anniversary Barbie, black,
    1997, No. 176608 . . . . .10 24
35th Anniversary Barbie, white,
    1997, No. 16485 . . . . .10 20
Baseball Date Barbie, 1993, No. 4583 . .10 30
City Style #1, 1996, No. 15612 . . . . . .8 15
City Style #2, 1997, No. 17237 . . . . . .10 20

Collector Editions & Store Exclusives

	MNB	MIB	Page #

Club Wedd Barbie, black,
    1998, No. 20423 . . . . .10 20
Club Wedd Barbie, blond or brunette,
    1998, No. 19717/19718 . . . . .10 20
Cute 'n Cool, 1991, No. 2954 . . . . .8 30
Dazzlin' Date Barbie, 1992, No. 3203 . .10 25
Easter Bunny Fun Barbie & Kelly,
    1999, No. 21720 . . . . .15 30
Easter Egg Hunt, 1998, No. 19014 . . . .15 40
Easter Egg Party, white or black, 2000 . .15 30
Easter Garden Hunt Barbie and Kelly,
    2001 . . . . .10 25
Gold and Lace Barbie, 1989, No. 7476 .10 30
Golden Evening, 1991, No. 2587 . . . . . .6 45
Golf Date Barbie, 1993, No. 10202 . . . .10 25
Halloween Fun Barbie & Kelly, white
    or black, 1999, No. 23460 . . . . . . .15 25
Halloween Fun Li'l Friends of Kelly,
    1999, No. 23796 . . . . .15 25
Halloween Party Barbie & Ken, pirates,
    1998, No. 19874 . . . . .20 40
Halloween Party Deidre (Pumpkin),
    2000, No. 28310 . . . . .5 15
Halloween Party Jenny (Pumpkin),
    2000, No. 28308 . . . . .5 15
Halloween Party Kayla (Ghost),
    2000, No. 28307 . . . . .5 15
Halloween Party Kelly (Alien),
    2000, No. 28306 . . . . .5 15
Halloween Party Tommy (Cowboy),
    2000, No. 28309 . . . . .5 15
Happy Halloween Barbie & Kelly,
    1997, No. 17238 . . . . .30 60
Party Pretty Barbie, 1990, No. 5955 . . . .6 25
Pet Doctor Barbie, brunette,
    1996, No. 16458 . . . . .15 30
Pretty in Plaid Barbie, 1992, No. 5413 .15 30
Soccer Kelly & Tommy, 1999 . . . . .8 20
Steppin' Out Barbie, 1995, No. 14110 . . .8 20
Valentine Barbie, 1996, No. 15172 . . . . .8 20
Valentine Date Barbie, 1998, No. 18306 .8 20
Valentine Kelly and Friend, 2001 . . . . . .5 15
Valentine Romance Barbie,
    1997, No. 16059 . . . . .8 20
Valentine Style Barbie, black,
    1999, No. 22150 . . . . .8 18
Valentine Style Barbie, white,
    1999, No. 20465 . . . . .8 15
Wild Style Barbie,
    1992, No. 0411 . . . . .10 24
With Love Barbie, 2000 . . . . .8 15
Xhilaration Barbie, white or black,
    1999 . . . . .15 35
Tennis Star Barbie & Ken,
    1988, No. 7801 . . . . .18 40
Tiff Pose N' Play, 1972, No. 1199 . . . .175 400

Timeless Sentiments
Angel of Hope, 1999, No. 22955 . . . . . .25 50
Angel of Joy, white or black,
    1998, No. 19633/20929 . . . . .25 50
Angel of Peace, white or black,
    1999, No. 24240/24241 . . . . .25 50
Todd Oldham (Designer), 1999 . . . . . . .35 70

Collector Editions & Store Exclusives

	MNB	MIB	Page #

Nostalgic Reproductions, 30th Anniversary Francie doll, 1996, $45 MIB

Collector Editions & Store Exclusives

	MNB	MIB	Page #

Collector Editions & Store Exclusives

	MNB	MIB	Page #

Police Officer Barbie, white,
1993, No. 10688 . . . . .15 70
Purple Passion, black,
1995, No. 13554 . . . . .10 30
Purple Passion, white,
1995, No. 13555 . . . . .10 30
Radiant in Red Barbie, black,
1992, No. 4113 . . . . .12 55
Radiant in Red Barbie, white,
1992, No. 1276 . . . . .12 55
Sapphire Sophisticate,
1997, No. 16692 . . . . .12 25
School Fun, 1991, No. 2721 . . . . .6 40
School Spirit Barbie, black,
1993, No. 10683 . . . . .10 30
School Spirit Barbie, white,
1993, No. 10682 . . . . .10 25
Share A Smile Barbie, 1997,
No. 17247 . . . . .7 15
Share A Smile Becky, 1997,
No. 15761 . . . . .15 28
Share A Smile Christie, 1997,
No. 17372 . . . . .7 15
Show and Ride Barbie, 1988,
No. 7799 . . . . .10 35
Sign Language Barbie, white or black,
2000 . . . . .8 20
Society Style Emerald Elegance,
1994, No. 12322 . . . . .15 40
Society Style Emerald Enchantment,
1997, No. 17443 . . . . .25 50
Society Style Sapphire Dream,
1995, No. 13256 . . . . .50 70
Space Camp Barbie, white or black,
1999, No. 22435/22246 . . . . .12 28
Spirit of the Earth Barbie, 2001 . . . . . .25 75
Spots 'N Dots Barbie, 1993, No. 10491 .12 35
Spots 'N Dots Teresa, 1993, No. 10885 .12 40
Spring Parade Barbie, white or black,
1992, No. 7008/2257 . . . . .15 30
Sunflower Barbie, 1995, No. 13488 . . . . .9 20
Sunflower Teresa, 1995, No. 13489 . . . . .9 20
Sweet Romance, 1991, No. 2917 . . . . . . .8 30
Sweet Roses, 1989, No. 7635 . . . . .7 25
Totally Hair Courtney, 1992, No. 1433 . .10 25
Totally Hair Skipper, 1992, No. 1430 . . .10 25
Totally Hair Whitney, 1992, No. 7735 . .20 40
Toys R Us/FAO Schwarz Sea
Holiday Barbie #1, with lip gloss,
1993 . . . . .15 30
Toys R Us/FAO Schwarz Sea
Holiday Barbie #2, with lip gloss,
1993 . . . . .15 24
Toys R Us/FAO/JCPenney, Winter
Sports Barbie, 1995 . . . . .15 30
Toys R Us/FAO/JCPenney, Winter
Sports Ken, 1995 . . . . .15 30
Travelin' Sisters Gift Set, 1995,
No. 14073 . . . . .30 65
Vacation Sensation Barbie, blue,
1986, No. 1675 . . . . .10 40
Vacation Sensation Barbie, pink,
1989, No. 1675 . . . . .12 48
Wedding Fantasy Barbie & Ken Gift Set,
1997, No. 17243 . . . . .20 45
Winter Fun Barbie, 1990, No. 5949 . . . .10 40

192-193

Collector Editions & Store Exclusives

	MNB	MIB	Page #

Toys R Us Harley-Davidson Barbie #3, 1999, $100 MIB

Collector Editions & Store Exclusives

	MNB	MIB	Page #

Trail Blazin' Barbie, 1991, No. 2783 . . .10 25
Tree Trimming Barbie, white or black,
1999 . . . . .5 15
Trend Forecaster Barbie,
1999, No. 22833 . . . . .20 45
Tropical Barbie Deluxe Gift Set,
1985, No. 2996 . . . . .20 45
Tutti and Todd Sundae Treat Set,
1966, No. 3556 . . . . .150 350
Tutti Me n' My Dog, 1966, No. 3554 . .150 350
Tutti Nighty Night Sleep Tight,
1965, No. 3553 . . . . .100 300
Twirley Curls Barbie Gift Set,
1982, No. 4097 . . . . .30 85

Twist and Turn Far Out Barbie,
1999, No. 21911 . . . . .20 40
Vera Wang #1, bride, 1998, No. 19788 . .75 150
Vera Wang #2, lavender dress,
1999, No. 23027 . . . . .55 140
Very Violet Barbie, 1992, No. 1859 . . . .10 20
Victorian Barbie with Cedric Bear,
2000 . . . . .25 59
Victorian Tea Orange Pekoe Barbie,
2000, No. 25507 . . . . .110 220
Walking Jamie Strollin'in Style Gift Set,
1972, No. 1247 . . . . .300 600

Wal-Mart
25th Year Pink Jubilee Barbie,
1987, No. 4589 . . . . .20 50
35th Anniversary Barbie, black or white,
No. 17616/17245 . . . . .10 24
35th Anniversary Teresa,
1997, No. 17617 . . . . .12 25
Anniversary Star Barbie, 1992,
No. 2282 . . . . .15 30
Ballroom Beauty, 1991, No. 3678 . . . . . .8 30
Bathtime Fun Barbie, 1991, No. 9601 . . .5 25
Country Bride, 1995, No. 13014 . . . . . .8 15
Country Bride, black, 1995, No. 13015 . .8 15
Country Bride, Hispanic,
1995, No. 13016 . . . . .8 15
Country Western Star Barbie, black or
Hispanic, 1994, No. 12096 . . . .12 30
Country Western Star Barbie, white,
1994, No. 12097 . . . . .10 25
Dream Fantasy, 1990, No. 7335 . . . . . . .8 35
Frills and Fantasy Barbie, 1988,
No. 1374 . . . . .7 45
Jewel Skating Barbie, 1999, No. 23239 . .6 12
Lavender Look Barbie, 1989, No. 3963 . .7 30
Portrait in Blue Barbie, black,
1998, No. 19356 . . . . .10 20
Portrait in Blue Barbie, white,
1998, No. 19355 . . . . .8 18
Pretty Choices Barbie, black,
1997, No. 18018 . . . . .8 18
Pretty Choices Barbie, blond or brunette,
1997, No. 17971/18019 . . . . .8 18
Puzzle Craze Barbie, white or black,
1998, No. 20164/20165 . . . . .6 14
Puzzle Craze Teresa, 1998, No. 20166 . . .6 14
Shopping Time Barbie, black or white,
1997, No. 18231/18230 . . . . .7 15

Collector Editions & Store Exclusives

	MNB	MIB	Page #

Shopping Time Teresa, 1997, No. 18232 .7 15
Skating Star Barbie, 1996, No. 15510 . .10 15
Star Skater Barbie, white or black, 2000 .5 15
Superstar Barbie, black, 1993,
No. 10711 . . . . .15 40
Superstar Barbie, white, 1993,
No. 10592 . . . . .15 30
Sweet Magnolia Barbie, black, white or
Hispanic, 1996,
No. 15653/15652/15654 . . . . .9 15
Tooth Fairy #1, 1994, No. 11645 . . . . . .7 20
Tooth Fairy #2, 1995, No. 11645 . . . . . .5 20
Tooth Fairy #3, 1998, No. 17246 . . . . . .6 14

Walt Disney World
Animal Kingdom Barbie, white or black,
1998, No. 20363/20989 . . . . .15 30
Barbie 25th Anniversary,
1996, No. 16525 . . . . .15 30
Disney Fun 1994, 1994, No. 11650 . . .15 50
Disney Fun 1995, 1995, No. 13533 . . .15 40
Disney Fun 1997, 1997, No. 17058 . . . .8 20
Millennium Barbie, white or black,
2000 . . . . .5 15
Resort Vacation Barbie, Ken,
Tommy, Kelly,
1998, No. 20315 . . . . .35 80
Toontown Stacie, 1994, No. 11587 . . . . .15 30

Warner Bros. Barbie Loves Tweety,
1999, No. 21632 . . . . .8 22
Warner Bros. Scooby-Doo Barbie,
2001, No. 27966 . . . . .5 15
Wedding Fantasy Gift Set,
1993, No. 10924 . . . . .50 125
Wedding Flower Blushing Orchid Bride,
1997 . . . . .100 200
Wedding Flower Romantic Rose Bride,
1996 . . . . .100 220
Wedding Party Gift Set, six dolls,
1991, No. 9852 . . . . .45 125
Wedgwood Barbie #1, blue dress,
2000, No. 25641 . . . . .40 80
Wedgwood Barbie #2, pink dress,
black, 2001, No. 50824 . . . . .30 85
Wedgwood Barbie #2, pink dress,
white, 2001, No. 50823 . . . . .30 85
Wessco Carnival Cruise Barbie,
1997, No. 15186 . . . . .25 40
Wessco International Traveler #1,
1995, No. 13912 . . . . .35 60
Wessco International Traveler #2,
1996, No. 16158 . . . . .25 50
Western Fun Gift Set Barbie & Ken,
1989, No. 5408 . . . . .12 30
Western Fun Gift Set Barbie & Ken,
1990, No. 5408 . . . . .12 30
Western Plains Barbie, 2000 . . . . .40 95
Winn-Dixie Party Pink Barbie,
1989, No. 7637 . . . . .7 25
Winn-Dixie Pink Sensation,
1990, No. 5410 . . . . .6 20
Winn-Dixie Southern Beauty,
1991, No. 3284 . . . . .10 25

Collector Editions & Store Exclusives

	MNB	MIB	Page #

Winter Princess #1 Winter Princess,
1993, No. 10655 . . . . .35 175
Winter Princess #2 Evergreen
Princess, 1994, No. 12123 . . . . . .35 100
Winter Princess #3 Peppermint
Princess, 1995, No. 13598 . . . . . .35 175
Winter Princess #4 Jewel Princess,
1996, No. 15826 . . . . .35 175
Winter Princess #5 Midnight Princess,
1997, No. 17780 . . . . .35 175

Woolworth's
Special Expressions, black, blue dress,
1991, No. 2583 . . . . .4 10
Special Expressions, black, peach dress,
1992, No. 3200 . . . . .5 30
Special Expressions, black, pink dress,
1990, No. 5505 . . . . .4 10
Special Expressions, black, white dress,
1989, No. 7326 . . . . .5 20
Special Expressions, blue dress, pastel
print, 1993, No. 10048 . . . . .5 15
Special Expressions, pink dress,
1990, No. 5504 . . . . .3 20
Special Expressions, white,
1989, No. 4842 . . . . .5 20
Special Expressions, white, blue dress,
1991, No. 2582 . . . . .4 15
Special Expressions, white, peach dress,
1992, No. 3197 . . . . .5 20
Sweet Lavender Barbie, black or white,
1992, No. 2523/2522 . . . . .12 28
Workin' Out Barbie Gift Set, 1997 . . . . .10 25
XXXOOO Barbie Doll , 2000 . . . . .8 20

Porcelain Barbie dolls

	MNB	MIB	Page #

30th Anniversary Ken, 1991, No. 1110 .75 175
30th Anniversary Midege, 1993, No.
7957 . . . . .65 150
30th Anniversary Skipper, 1994,
No. 11396 . . . . .50 150
Benefit Performance Barbie,
1988, No. 5475 . . . . .200 425
Blue Rhapsody, first porcelain Barbie,
1986, No. 1708 . . . . .300 600
Blushing Orchid Bride Barbie,
1997, No. 16962 . . . . .75 175

Bob Mackie Celebration of Dance
Charleston, 2001 . . . . .100 300
Tango, 1999, No. 23451 . . . . .150 200

Crystal Rhapsody, blond, Presidential
Porcelain Barbie collection,
1992, No. 1553 . . . . .100 300
Crystal Rhapsody, brunette, Presidential
Porcelain Barbie collection,
1993, No. 10201 . . . . .100 600

Porcelain Barbie dolls

	MNB	MIB	Page #

Enchanted Evening Barbie,
1987, No. 3415 . . . . .175 400
Faberge Imperial Elegance Barbie,
limited to 15,000, 1999,
No. 19816 . . . . .150 350
Gay Parisienne, blond, 1991,
No. 9973 . . . . .225 625
Gay Parisienne, brunette, 1991,
No. 9973 . . . . .150 225
Gay Parisienne, redhead, 1991,
No. 9973 . . . . .225 625
Gold Sensation, Gold and Silver
Porcelain Barbie Set, 1993,
No. 10246 . . . . .175 350

Holiday Porcelain
#1, Holiday Jewel, 1995, No. 14311 . . .55 225
#2, Holiday Caroler, 1996, No. 15760 . .60 200
#3, Holiday Ball, 1997, No. 18326 . . . . .75 200
#4, Holiday Gift, 1998, No. 20128 . . . .100 200

Mattel's 50th Anniversary Barbie,
1995, No. 14479 . . . . .300 . . .350
Mint Memories, Victorian Tea
Porcelain Collection, 1999 . . . . . .100 215
Plantation Belle, blond, Porcelain
Treasures Collection, 1992,
No. 7526 . . . . .100 575
Plantation Belle, red, Porcelain
Treasures Collection, 1992,
No. 5351 . . . . .100 200
Presidential Porcelain Evening
Pearl Barbie, 1996 . . . . .95 225
Romantic Rose Bride, 1995, No. 14541 .75 175
Royal Splendor, Presidential
Porcelain Collection, 1993,
No. 10950 . . . . .100 250

Silken Flame, brunette,
Porcelain Treasures Collection,
1993, No. 1249 . . . . .100 200
Silken Flame, blond, 1993,
No. 11099 . . . . .250 500
Silver Starlight, Gold and Silver
Porcelain Barbie Set, 1994,
No. 11875 . . . . .175 350
Solo in the Spotlight, 1990, No. 7613 . .100 200
Sophisticated Lady, 1990, No. 5313 . . .125 200
Star Lily Bride Barbie, Wedding
Flower Collection, 1995,
No. 12953 . . . . .125 250
Wedding Day Barbie, 1989, No. 2641 .300 400

Wizard of Oz
Dorothy, 2000, No. 26834 . . . . .70 150
Scarecrow, 2001, No. 29190 . . . . .50 150
Tin Man, 2001, No. 29676 . . . . .50 150
Wicked Witch, 2000, No. 26835 . . . . . .70 150
Winged Monkey, 2001, No. 29476 . . . . .50 150

Together Forever, Barbie and Ken as Romeo and Juliet, 1998, $100 MIB

Ponytail #1, 1959
Current Value: **$9,000 MIB**